Almighty God says, "Quit your worship charades. I can't stand your trivial religious games. Monthly conferences, weekly Sabbaths, special meetings— meetings, meetings, meetings—I can't stand one more! "Meetings for this, meetings for that. I hate them. You've worn me out. I'm sick of your religion, religion, religion, while you go right on sinning."

– Isaiah 1:13-17 (MSG)

THE HIDDEN TRUTH

For Those Who Know There's More

Than the Church Teaches

Jon Dean Smith

Donna Louise Smith

Copyright © Lynn Baber 2019

All rights reserved.

No part of this book may be used or reproduced by any means without the express written permission from Lynn Baber.

ISBN 978-1-938836-31-2

Published by Ark Press

Texas, United States

All Scripture quotations, unless otherwise indicated, are taken from the Holy Bible, New International Version®, NIV®. Copyright ©1973, 1978, 1984, 2011 by Biblica, Inc.™ Used by permission of Zondervan. All rights reserved worldwide. The "NIV" and "New International Version" are trademarks registered in the United States Patent and Trademark Office by Biblica, Inc.™

Jon Dean and Donna Smith express their appreciation to Jeritt and Merritt King for their 180 descriptive sentences of Christlike maturity in The Hidden Truth. Used with permission.

Originally published as Please Become Our Disciple! in 2014.

Foreword by Lynn Baber

There is no lovelier and peaceful place than the center of God's will; wrapped in wisdom, secure in the knowledge of your home in eternity, and feeling nothing more stressful than the soft breeze of the Holy Spirit.

Peace. Joy. Soul rest. Few churches teach members how to experience—to live—the blessing of Jesus's promises. If you're like most self-labeled Christians, these promises from Jesus Christ are concepts or hopes, not your everyday reality as it can be.

Millions of people accept Christ, wait for a life transformation that doesn't come, then wonder, "Is this all there is?" For those brave enough to ask, the answers seldom suffice. No word of man can bring the perfect peace Jesus promises. Faith, joy, and fearlessness are gifts of the Holy Spirit, not the cumulative result of scholarship or service.

Authors Jon Dean (JD) and Donna Smith live in soul rest, a testimony to the truth of the gospel, considering the severity of the testing they've endured. JD is an unusual man. He is fully Christ's man, something many believe about themselves, but their thoughts and behaviors suggest otherwise.

At first, I wasn't sure if I believed what I heard from JD and Donna. That wasn't an issue until they invited my husband and me to enter into discipleship with them. Three months into our study and conversations, JD had a routine MRI to evaluate a frozen shoulder that revealed suspicious lesions on his lungs and thyroid. The doctor said they appeared cancerous but would wait for the pathology report before making a final diagnosis.

Donna suffers from advanced Parkinson's Disease and requires constant help, a service JD has joyfully given for two decades. If this was cancer, their most reasonable option was moving closer to their son's family for help with Donna. Daily text messages and bi-weekly meetings with JD and Donna kept my husband and me in the loop of test results and their daily needs and spiritual condition.

Every day was the same. "We are at peace."

On Monday, the pathology report confirmed the initial opinion; JD had terminal lung cancer. They decided to move west to be with their son, Jon Alan. Two days later, Jon Alan underwent emergency surgery for brain lesions and soon passed into the presence of his beloved Savior. JD and Donna would stay where they were.

Every day the message was the same, "We are at peace."

Doctors told JD he might live two years with treatment and one year without. Any significant treatment would take away his ability to care for Donna. Together, JD and Donna chose not to treat.

We sat with them, prayed with them, studied with them, and learned with them. They mourned their son's loss, but with joy, hope, and perfect peace.

JD and Donna are for real.

Over the next fifteen months, we worked on this second edition of their book and made plans for me to continue building on the foundation they laid throughout decades of discipleship, ministry, and obedience.

Can you trust what JD and Donna write? Yes. Not because they're amazing, but because what they share in *The Hidden Truth* is purely Jesus's message, His ministry, His teaching, and His promises. What makes them unique is that they believe it, live it and bask in joy and peace that passes earthly understanding.

So can you. JD and Donna Smith wrote this book to help you through the discovery and discipleship process they documented and taught. This updated edition of their 2014 book makes is easier for readers to use and apply. Both the book and the life we've shared with the Smiths over the past twenty months illustrate Relational Discipleship; walking together in Christ.

Jesus says, "If you love Me, keep My commandments." (John 14:15)

What does Jesus command? What does He promise to the obedient? *The Hidden Truth* clearly lays out both His commands and promises (Chapter 11).

We are called to daily become more like Christ. But what is He like? *The Hidden Truth* offers one-hundred eighty characteristics of Christ (Chapter 10).

More churches teach congregational doctrine, service, and opinion than teach Jesus. *The Hidden Truth* is 100% Jesus; who He is, how He taught His disciples, what He both promises and commands, and what you can expect from walking daily in the Holy Spirit.

Yes, the Holy Spirit, the one Person of the Trinity seldom taught in mainline churches. If you're not intimately related to this member of the Godhead, you miss the vital connection that makes Jesus real in your life today. Transformation is only possible through the Spirit of God.

The Hidden Truth is pro-church; the church that Jesus will greet with joy and love when He returns. Most churches are institutions of man, not discipling centers based on what Jesus lived and taught. Life mixes strife, conflict, and fear among beauty and blessings. God the Father created the human spirit to seek truth, but we don't always recognize it. True soul rest becomes possible when the Spirit of God in you discerns what is real.

Does your church teach what Jesus taught His disciples? Are the people you gather with progressively moving to higher levels of confidence in Christ? Do they make disciples of others?

"Jesus Christ is the same yesterday, today, and tomorrow." (Hebrews 13:8) He does not evolve, adapt, or morph. Jesus is God, unchangeable and uncompromising.

What did Jesus teach? He taught love, obedience, and community.

Living in the light and power of all that's possible in Christ is unimaginable to most who warm pews in western congregations because they are limited to well-intentioned and educated but uninspired messages from the pulpit. Here is the opportunity to study what Jesus taught, and then compare what you know today with what God's Word holds for you.

Welcome to *The Hidden Truth*.

Table of Contents

Foreword by Lynn Baber..7

Table of Contents..11

Preface from the Authors...13

Part One: The Kingdom of God..17

Chapter 1–The Two Spiritual Kingdoms......................................21

Chapter 2–A Short History of God's Covenants........................23

Part Two: Welcome to the New Covenant Care of God's Family..31

Chapter 3: Training Spiritual Babies and Infants to Become Victorious Kingdom Workers..33

Chapter 4: Jesus Christ's Five Foundational Elementary Basics.....35

Chapter 5: Introduction to The Lifetime Terms of the New Covenant..37

Chapter 6: Relational Discipleship, the Teaching-Learning Model for Disciples of Jesus Christ..39

Chapter 7: Counting the Cost to Be Jesus Christ's Disciple..........41

Chapter 8: A Life of Relational Discipleship..............................45

Part Three: The Lifetime Terms of the New Covenant..............61

Chapter 9 – New Covenant Term One..63

Chapter 10– New Covenant Term Two......................................69

Chapter 11– New Covenant Terms Three and Four..................83

Chapter 12– New Covenant Term Five 123

Part Four: Some Victory Principles of the Kingdom of God 135

Chapter 13: Soul Rest to Hear the Holy Spirit 137

Chapter 14: God's Five-Step Power Sin Wash..........................141

Chapter 15: My Special Tool Design Made in His Image 145

Chapter 16: Gentle Restoration—God's Way to Wash Away Sin-Guilt 155

Chapter 17: Mending Broken Hearts..159

Chapter 18: Endurance for Persecution...165

Chapter 19: Three Power Authorizations 171

Chapter 20: Spiritual Warfare by the New Covenanters............177

Chapter 21: God's Four-Step Health Plan...................................183

Chapter 22: Learning to Love the Fear of God 189

Chapter 23: Perfect Peace from the Prince of Peace...................191

Chapter 24: What We Gain by Giving Up Everything To Follow Jesus Christ 193

Part Five: Our Eyewitness Testimony – Some of God's Amazing Deeds on Our Journey 197

Co-Authors' Conclusions 239

About the Authors...241

Preface from the Authors

Welcome to *The Hidden Truth*, our eye-witness report of what God has revealed to us about relational discipleship for the past sixty years. Here are many proven lessons, spiritual routines, scripture lists and stories designed for you to read and consider. We invite you to share the truth that enables individuals to:

- Become like Jesus Christ.
- Daily live like Jesus Christ.
- Experience Jesus Christ's complete joy.

I was sent into revival ministry in 1957 and almighty God blessed me with my beloved wife Donna in 1962. For years I taught and preached the gospel I learned from my church leaders and the Jesus Christ that my family and church leaders introduced to me, but I knew little about the Holy Spirit of God.

In 1969, I was burdened about not bringing Christlike maturity to the precious people around me. I poured out my heart to almighty God in a church broom closet in West Texas with this request, *Dear Lord, something is missing in the Christianity that we know. Please show me what it is. I seek the Christlike maturity that I see in the New Testament of the Bible. Show me what I need to know, and I will attempt to share it with my friends. Amen.*

It was my application of Jeremiah 33:3.

In 1971, God began answering my prayer by intentionally moving my family to five cities and putting into my heart the real Bible truths that I missed about Christianity. It was eight years of Kingdom of God revelations that I never knew before. This was my application of Isaiah 1:7-10.

Then in 1978, heavenly Father brought us back to the same town where we started to share the true biblical Christian lifestyle we had learned. These results brought much glory to almighty God for over twenty years, as many local cities witnessed true biblical Christianity.

Many individuals were touched, and our Disciples Journal went around the world.

Since returning to the Fort Worth area in 1999, heavenly Father continued expanding our quiet biblical lifestyle. The evidence of mature Christlike men and women in normal life proves the power of what we share in this book. The rich relationships that almighty God developed with many men and women since we began studying and implementing three elements, have resulted in wonderful peace-filled kingdom of God dominion over the forces of evil in measurable practical ways.

The elements that make up this wonderful rich practical and transferable life on Earth are (1) the New Covenant of Jesus Christ, (2) the kingdom of almighty God, and (3) relational discipleship taught by Jesus of Nazareth.

We are delighted to report the results of applying what we've learned through Jesus Christ's life and His teaching. We introduce people into the New Covenant through Relational Discipleship. The amazing truths found by careful biblical examination of what Jesus Christ did with his own disciples resulted in positive Christlike maturity in the men and women who became our disciples, training themselves to become disciple makers for Jesus Christ. God then brought others to them, and they fulfilled Matthew 28:19-20.

Consider the significant scriptural revelation that Jesus Christ authorized, and how He commanded His apostles to make disciples instead of building His church.

Jesus makes these four points in the Gospel of John, chapters 17 and 18:

#1. Jesus revealed to His disciples who almighty God really is.

#2. Jesus confirmed that His disciples obeyed everything that the heavenly Father gave Him to teach.

#3. Jesus's disciples believed that God sent Jesus to be their disciple maker.

#4. Jesus sent them out to make other disciple makers (to reproduce these four same things).

The Bible teaches that Jesus's reason for coming to the earth was to make almighty God's truth on every subject prevail over Satan's lies by bringing God's truth to this world (John 18:36–37), by placing His Spirit of Truth within the heart of each obedient Christian (John 14:15–17; 2 Corinthians 1:21–23), and teaching us how to become competent ministers of the New Covenant as living letters from Christ (2 Corinthians 3:3–6).

In this book, you will discover almighty God's plans for you to become an effective spiritual workman through whom God consistently places His kingdom and His will in the earth—without offending others.

You will learn to:

- Identify and accomplish God's pre-planned daily work.
- Establish fairness (justice) and excellence (righteousness).
- Dispel evil and darkness.
- Earn respect
- Share your success-secrets when asked.
- Receive almighty God's "Well done."

The kingdom of God is the primary subject that Jesus Christ and the apostles established on the Earth. Jesus's lessons to His disciples still apply today. They will empower you to change your portion of the world for Jesus Christ.

It is amazing how being in the New Covenant of almighty God enables His sons and daughters to affect spiritual conditions wherever they are. Chapter 20, *Spiritual Warfare by the New Covenanters*, provides a biblical understanding of the unseen spiritual conflict going on in your life right now.

Jesus Christ's commission was accomplished through my life in much the same way Jesus Christ reported it in His life.

Simply stated, doing what Jesus taught, it is this:

1. I have mature Christlike friends who know whom almighty God truly is.
2. I observe these disciples of Jesus Christ obeying the same commands Jesus taught his disciples to obey.
3. My disciples understand that it was God who sent me to them, becoming my trusted friends and productive Kingdom co-workers.
4. I sent them into the world to make more disciple makers for Jesus Christ.

Today my greatest joy is seeing these friends living so much in the image of Christ that almighty God brings them disciples. Our disciple's lives demonstrate an amazing spiritual dominion right where they live and work in the earth.

We offer you this Biblical rediscovery, *The Hidden Truth*, of the faith that Jesus Christ and His apostles originally placed in the earth. (Jude 1:3–5). As you will read, almighty God revealed two components of the faith that Jesus Christ and his apostles brought to the Earth.

1. The actual terms of The New Covenant, and
2. How to make disciples like Jesus made his disciples.

Personally, our deepest delight is worshipping almighty God in the way that He seeks, *in Spirit and in truth* and walking in daily soul rest (John 4:23–24).

Jon Dean and Donna Smith

Part One: The Kingdom of God

The spiritual Kingdom of God, also called the Kingdom of Heaven, is the eternal spiritual government over almighty God's creation, with Jesus Christ as King of Kings. The Lord God Almighty is the Eternal Creator, who originally placed His will and kingdom on the earth through the first human beings who were created in His image. Adam and Eve received clear instruction to rule the earth with the powerful authority they received from God.

Their life and work agreement (the first covenant with humanity) explained the terms of God's covenant. The man and woman clearly understood what to do and what not to do. God also warned them what would happen if they disobeyed the terms of the covenant.

With their complete dominion and authority over the earth, Eden was a perfect extension of God's will and kingdom. For a period of time, it was very fulfilling and rewarding to them. Can you imagine the awesome experience of naming every animal and enjoying daily fellowship with almighty God? Yet Adam and Eve messed up, inciting a war.

There is presently a largely unseen spiritual war between Creator God and the rebellious angel, Satan. This ancient war ends with God's total vengeance and victory (Hebrews 10:26–31; 2 Peter 2:13) and with a new heaven and new earth (Isaiah 65:17, 66:22; 2 Peter 3:13; Revelation 21:1).

Humanity Surrendered Spiritual Authority to Satan

Biblical history shows that Adam and Eve chose to do what they desired instead of obeying God. When offered a choice by the deceiver-serpent, they broke humanity's first covenant from God. The consequences of breaking God's covenant brought His curses and the removal of their authority over the earth. They even disregarded God's warning of their own death. (Genesis 3:16–19; Hosea 6:7). At that time, Satan-the devil took the earth into his kingdom of darkness.

The apostle John comments on Satan's control of the world, "We know that we are children of God and that all the rest of the world around us is under Satan's power and control" (1 John 5:19, TLB).

Satan declared his authority and splendor during Jesus's wilderness testing. "The devil led him up to a high place and showed him in an instant all the kingdoms of the world. And he said to him, "I will give you all their authority and splendor; it has been given to me, and I can give it to anyone I want to. If you worship me, it will all be yours" (Luke 4:5–7).

The Spiritual War Continues Today Until Jesus Christ Comes in Victory

Almighty God started this spiritual war in the Garden of Eden as a consequence and curse upon rebellious angels and human beings who broke their God-given covenant assignments (Genesis 3:14–15), which is clearly described by Jesus's apostles in 1 John 5:18–19, Ephesians 6:10–18, and 1 Peter 5:11. Christ will physically come to earth for a thousand-year reign (Revelation 20), which will end when Jesus Christ presents His complete victory to almighty God (Revelation 20:7–10; 1 Corinthians 15:24–28).

The Kingdom of God Today

God's spiritual Kingdom is now on the earth within almighty God's New Covenant members. King Jesus Christ presently rules God's kingdom from His heavenly throne (Matthew 19:28, 20:23, 25:31; Revelation 3:21, 19:16; John 18:36–37; 1 Corinthians 15:24–28), by the spiritual instructions He gives God's sons and daughters through the Holy Spirit (Romans 8:4–16; Galatians 5:16, 25).

Jesus Christ introduced almighty God's New Covenant, became its crucified sacrificial lamb, was resurrected from the grave, and provided an additional forty days of kingdom instruction. After His ascension to heaven, He completed his first-coming world duties by pouring out the Holy Spirit on the earth. Recorded in Acts chapter 2, the Kingdom of God was officially released through the apostles into the earth at the Jewish feast of Pentecost.

What Today's Church Doesn't Know

Sadly, the Bible reports that the original faith was largely lost in the early church period. (Jude 3–5; 2 Corinthians 11:3–4.) But, with great joy and humility we share with you significant portions of that original faith that bring the Kingdom of God victory into real-life situations. This is *The Hidden Truth*.

In this book, we gladly present real-life steps to be spiritually victorious every day.

Chapter 1–The Two Spiritual Kingdoms

In this book, you will learn how to remain victorious in the present continuous spiritual conflict between Satan-the devil and almighty God-the Creator. The amazing reality for the New Covenant minister in the Earth today is how he or she can walk, talk, and respond to every issue the same way Jesus Christ did.

Every person on earth is a citizen of some earthly government made up of land boundaries with various laws and regulations. All humans are subjects living within a spiritual kingdom, dominated by a spiritual ruler or king. The first is the kingdom of darkness ruled by Satan. He is the evil spiritual prince of this world, also called the ruler of the kingdom of the air and the god of this age (Genesis 3:14–15; John 4:10–11, 12:31, 14:30; Ephesians 2:2).

The second spiritual kingdom is the Kingdom of God, which was reestablished in the earth by King Jesus Christ who said, "My kingdom is not of this world. But now my kingdom is from another place. In fact, the reason I was born and came into the world is to testify to the truth. Everyone on the side of truth listens to me" (John 18:36–37).

There is much to learn about the Kingdom of God and the covenants offered to humanity. Presently in the earth, the Kingdom of God, embodied by the Holy Spirit of God, is within the heart of each member of God's New Covenant. God's plan is for each one in His spiritual family to become more like Jesus Christ and be victorious over the devil's agents.

This spiritual war rages as you read this book.

"Be alert and of sober mind. Your enemy the devil prowls around like a roaring lion looking for someone to devour. Resist him, standing firm in the faith, because you know that the family of believers throughout the world is undergoing the same kind of sufferings" (1 Peter 5:8–9).

"Finally, be strong in the Lord and in his mighty power. Put on the full armor of God, so that you can take your stand against the devil's schemes. For our struggle is not against flesh and blood, but against the rulers, against the authorities, against the powers of this dark world and against the spiritual forces of evil in the heavenly realms. Therefore, put on the full armor of God, so that when the day of evil comes, you may be able to stand your ground" (Ephesians 6:10–13).

Presently in the unseen third heaven, the Kingdom of God expands each time a faithful New Covenanter finishes his or her earthly duty and is welcomed into heavenly Father's arms. At almighty God's appointed time, as King of the Kingdom of God, the Lord Jesus Christ with His called, chosen and faithful workers will return to this earth to rule and reign, dominating the kingdom of darkness on this earth.

At almighty God's signal, the earth will be removed, and every human will experience God's eternal judgment; either eternal life with God in His kingdom on the New Earth or eternal death with Satan in his kingdom in the lake of fire.

Chapter 2–A Short History of God's Covenants

God loved mankind so much that He offered a variety of covenants. God's *Edenic covenant* with the original man and woman before their sin, reveals God's original purpose for the human race (Genesis 1).

After Adam and Eve committed the original sin, God's *Adamic covenant* revealed His verdict on sin and also guaranteed a redeemer-Messiah (Genesis 3). After the flood, God's *Noahic covenant* with Noah included all of earth's creation, creatures, future humanity, and confirmed God's purposes from the Edenic covenant (Genesis 6:18, 9:8–18).

God's *Abrahamic covenant* with Abraham (Isaac and Jacob) after the Tower of Babel and the scattering of the sons of Noah into tongues, families, and nations, set up Israel. Abraham's natural and national seed identified God's people and Jesus Christ as their Messiah. Both Israelites and Gentiles were offered this covenant into the kingdom of God (Genesis 12:1–3, 15:18–21, 17:1–27).

God's Mt. Sinai *Mosaic covenant* through Moses, with the nation of Israel after the Exodus from Egypt, was designed as an instructive preparation for Israel to welcome the Savior of the world, Jesus Christ (Exodus 19–30; Galatians 3:24). God's *Palestinian covenant* was made through Moses with the younger generation of Israel. After forty years of wilderness wanderings before entering Canaan, the Abrahamic covenant land, the Palestinian covenant offered God's terms for entering and maintaining the Promised Land (Deuteronomy Chapters 27–33).

After the death of King Saul, God's *Davidic covenant* with David established the Davidic kingdom line, including Jesus Christ, the King of Kings and Lord of Lords (2 Samuel 7; Psalms 89 and 132).

God's *New Covenant* presented by Jesus Christ to Israel and Judah was officially rejected by the Jewish leaders, who continued the old Mosaic covenant. The few who accepted the New Covenant received God's Holy Spirit and established the Bride of Christ (the church). These were the first ministers of the New Covenant (Jeremiah 31:31–34; Ezekiel 36:25–27; Matthew 26:26–29; Luke 22:20; Hebrews 8:6–13, 10:16, 17, 29, 12:24, 13:20; Acts 2; 2 Corinthians 3:6).

The New Covenant Is the Only Way to Enter the Kingdom of God

"This is the covenant I will establish with the people of Israel after that time, declares the Lord. I will put my laws in their minds and write them on their hearts. I will be their God, and they will be my people. No longer will they teach their neighbor, or say to one another, 'Know the Lord,' because they will all know me, from the least of them to the greatest. For I will forgive their wickedness and will remember their sins no more. By calling this covenant "new," he has made the first one obsolete; and what is obsolete and outdated will soon disappear" (Hebrews 8:10–13; also Ezekiel 36:25–27; Hebrews 9:14–15).

The way for each human to get right with God, enter into the New Covenant, and stay on the right path until their earthly life ends, is to maintain their faith in God and obey what Jesus taught His disciples. The narrow path of keeping the terms of the New Covenant until one's mortal death leads to eternal life.

More New Covenant Information

The teaching and learning process that Jesus Christ and the apostles offered was personal discipleship. The processes we label mentoring or internship are similar in practice. Disciple makers answer all questions and provide Kingdom of God perspectives about every issue of real life they face together. In this book we call this process Relational Discipleship (RD).

Relational Discipleship is a spiritual family support system which facilitates both the entrance into the New Covenant and the daily obedience of the covenant terms. Disciples agree to study, understand, and obey the terms of God's New Covenant all the days of their earthly lives. All agree to confess their significant sins to almighty God before a spiritual family member who spiritually washes their feet and robes, by confirming Father's forgiveness and spiritual restoration. That process is explained later in this book.

New Covenant terms should be taught regularly within each home. Every item and situation of daily life is evaluated through Kingdom of God truths.

Warning: God Wants Clean, Righteous Men and Women

Almighty God says, "Quit your worship charades. I can't stand your trivial religious games. Monthly conferences, weekly Sabbaths, special meetings— meetings, meetings, meetings—I can't stand one more! Meetings for this, meetings for that. I hate them. You've worn me out. I'm sick of your religion, religion, religion, while you go right on sinning. When you put on your next prayer-performance, I'll be looking the other way. No matter how long or loud or often you pray, I'll not be listening. And do you know why? Because you've been tearing people to pieces, and your hands are bloody. Go home and wash up. Clean up your act. Sweep your lives clean of your evildoing so I don't have to look at them any longer. Say no to wrong. Learn to do good. Work for justice. Help the down-and-out. Stand up for the homeless. Go to bat for the defenseless" (Isaiah 1:17–19 MSG).

Some New Covenant Rewards and Consequences

Believers earn various rewards by their faith-filled obedience and keeping covenant. One who obediently believes that God sent Jesus as the Savior and keeps the covenant, crosses from eternal death into eternal life (John 3:14–15, 5:24).

One who blesses Jesus's disciples in His name will be eternally rewarded (Matthew 10:40–42; Mark 9:41).

As a New Covenant member, you can gain various ranks in the kingdom of God:

- Entry rank (Matthew 7:21–23, 18:3, 19:17, 23)

- First rank (Matthew 19:30, 20:16; Mark 9:35, 10:31; Luke 13:30)
- Great rank (Matthew 5:19, 18:4; Mark 10:43–44; Luke 22:26–27)
- Judge throne rank (Matthew 19:28; Luke 22:28–30)
- Last rank (Matthew 19:30, 20:16)
- Least rank (Matthew 5:19)
- Jesus's left throne rank (Matthew 20:21–23; Mark 10:35–40)
- Perfect rank (Matthew 5:48, 19:21)
- Jesus's right throne rank (Matthew 20:23; Mark 10:39–40)

Additional rewards are earned from your faith-filled obedience:

- God honors those servants of Jesus who follow His lifestyle (John 12:25–26).
- Great blessings come from making lasting disciple fruit, including significant prayer answers (John 15:7–17).
- Heavenly treasure is stored up by obeying Jesus's commands (Matthew 6:19–21; Luke 12:33–34).
- Helping the least of these brings my own eternal kingdom (Matthew 25:31–46; John 5:28–29).
- I expect, "Well done ... put you in charge ... share master's happiness" (Matthew 25:20–23; Mark 13:34; Luke 19:17).
- I look forward to taking my own kingdom that was prepared for me (Matthew 19:28, 25:34; Luke 22:28–30).
- If I keep the covenant until my life end, Jesus will gather and protect me (Matthew 3:12, 13:30).
- Jesus promised rewards for His disciples (John 14:1–4).
- Jesus greatly rewards those who leave everything to follow Him (Matthew 19:27–30).
- Jesus's story of the talents is about rewards and consequences (Matthew 25:14–30).
- My own eternal rewards will be what I deserve from my life choices/actions (Matthew 16:27; Revelations 20:11–14, 22:12).

- Daily obeying Jesus, grasping my own cross, and losing my life for His name gain me eternal rewards (Matthew 10:38, 16:24; Luke 9:23, 14:25–27; John 12:25–26).
- When I fulfill my part, great blessings can be mine (Matthew 5:3–12; Luke 6:17–26).

Various Consequences Are Received from One's Disobedience (From Breaking Covenant):

- Causing one to sin brings a terrible penalty (Matthew 18:6–9; Mark 9:42–50; Luke 17:1–4).
- Sons in God's Kingdom can be recognized by their fruit (Matthew 13:24–43; John 8:42–47).
- Disobedient servants of Jesus will miss heaven (Matthew 25:26–30; Luke 12:46–47).
- Doing ministry in Jesus's name without being known by Him receives, "Depart from me" (Matthew 7:21–23; Luke 13:25–27).
- Faithless, disobedient subjects of the Kingdom of God are thrown out (Matthew 8:5–13).
- False leaders and their followers will fall into a pit (Matthew 15:1–20; Luke 7:1–23).
- Foolish ones who are not ready for Jesus will not get into heaven (Matthew 25:8–13, 24:42, 50).
- God will separate the wicked out of the Kingdom of Heaven (Matthew 13:49–50, 13:41, 25:32).
- God's wrath remains on everyone who rejects Jesus Christ (John 3:36).
- Hypocrites miss heaven (Matthew 23:1–33; Mark 12:37–40; Luke 20:45–47).
- I can cause my own forgiveness from God to be removed (Matthew 18:21–35).
- If I continually disobey, Jesus will burn me like a weed (Matthew 3:12; Luke 3:17).
- If I continue to sin, I will miss heaven (Matthew 5:27–30).
- If I disconnect from Jesus, my salt source, I become a good-for-nothing throw-out (Matthew 5:13; Mark 9:50; Luke 14:34).

- If I disown Jesus before men, He will disown me before the heavenly Father (Matthew 10:33; Mark 8:38).
- If I do not produce kingdom fruit, I will end miserably (Matthew 21:41–45, 8:12; Mark 12:9; Luke 20:16).
- If I find fulfillment in anything other than Jesus Christ, I will miss heaven (Matthew 10:39; Mark 8:35; Luke 9:24; John 12:25).
- If I refuse to forgive others, my guilt remains upon me (Matthew 6:14–15; 18:32–35).
- If I separate myself from Jesus Christ, the Vine, I will miss heaven (John 15:6).
- If I stop obeying and loving Jesus Christ, I will miss heaven (Matthew 10:37; Luke 14:26).
- Major warnings apply to anyone who remains in sin (Matthew 18:7–9).
- Many who did many miracles in the name of Jesus and were unforgiven for doing evil will hear, "I never knew you, away from me" (Matthew 7:22–23).
- Many who cast out demons in the name of Jesus but were unforgiven for doing evil will hear, "I never knew you, away from me" (Matthew 7:22–23).
- Many who had prophesied in the name of Jesus but were unforgiven for doing evil will hear, "I never knew you, away from me" (Matthew 7:22–23).
- My careless words condemn me (Matthew 12:36–37).
- My deeds done for men's approval are of no value (Matthew 6:1–4).
- Not putting Jesus Christ's words into practice brings my life crashing down (Matthew 7:26; Luke 6:47–49).
- Not being spiritually dressed (in Christ's righteousness) (Matthew 22:13, 8:12).
- Refusing to faithfully obey causes God's sons and daughters to miss heaven (Matthew 8:5–13; Luke 13:28–29, 14:24).
- Serious consequences of the tenant's story apply today (Matthew 21:33–42; Mark 12:1–12).
- Some miss heaven by thinking they are saved by their Bible studies (John 5:39).

- The kingdom of God is removed from Jesus's fruitless servants (Matthew 21:43–46).
- The majority will miss heaven (Matthew 7:13-14, 8:12, 21:41–43, 22:11–14; Luke 13:23–24, 28, 14:24).
- The penalty for contemptuous and insulting words is missing heaven (Matthew 5:22).
- The warning is that all people need to live repentant, sin-washed lives (Matthew 11:20–24).
- Those who did not meet the needs of the least will go to eternal punishment (Matthew 25:41–46).
- Wicked servants of Jesus will be where there is weeping and gnashing of teeth (Matthew 24:51; Luke 12:45–48).
- Worthless servants of Jesus are thrown outside into darkness with weeping and gnashing of teeth (Luke 19:20–27; Matthew 25:24–30).

Part Two: Welcome to the New Covenant Care of God's Family

Human and spiritual babies both need the same three basic provisions. In a perfect world, every baby would be in daily close relationship with its parents who provide: (1) correct feeding, (2) correct cleaning and (3) correct resting, which then result in healthy maturity.

In a manner of speaking, Jesus Christ stayed close to his twelve spiritual babies in similar ways. Within their relational discipleship, Jesus daily provided spiritual feeding, spiritual cleaning and spiritual resting. We present Jesus's three basic spiritual provisions in the following chapters:

Correct feeding: "Like newborn babies, crave pure spiritual milk, so that by it you may grow up in your salvation" (1 Peter 2:2). See Chapters 3 through 24.

Correct cleaning: "Now that I, your Lord and Teacher, have washed your feet, you also should wash one another's feet" (John 13:14). See Chapter 16: *Gentle Restoration and* Chapter 14: *God's Five-Step Power Sin Wash.*

Correct resting: "Take my yoke upon you and learn from me, for I am gentle and humble in heart, and you will find rest for your souls" (Matthew 11:29). See Chapter 13: *Soul Rest and* Chapter 23: *Perfect Peace from the Prince of Peace.*

Chapter 3: Training Spiritual Babies and Infants to Become Victorious Kingdom Workers

God always deals with humans through the covenants (agreements) that He offers them. Almighty God, the Creator of the universe, today offers a lifetime agreement or covenant (work contract) to each human.

"This is the covenant I will establish with the people. I will put my laws in their minds and write them on their hearts. I will be their God, and they will be my people. They will all know me, from the least of them to the greatest. For I will forgive their wickedness and will remember their sins no more" (Hebrews 8:10–12).

"While they were eating, Jesus took bread, and when he had given thanks, he broke it and gave it to his disciples, saying, "Take and eat; this is my body." Then he took a cup, and when he had given thanks, he gave it to them, saying, "Drink from it, all of you. This is my blood of the covenant, which is poured out for many for the forgiveness of sins" (Matthew 26:26–28).

Kingdom of God Spiritual Caregivers

Jesus Christ wants each new disciple to have a disciple maker; "Make disciples in all the nations ... and then teach these new disciples to obey all the commands I have given you" (Matthew 28:19–20 NLT).

Each person enters into the kingdom of God as a spiritual baby no matter what physical age they are when he or she decides to enter the New Covenant. The Bible uses the spiritual terms babies, infants, children, youths, fathers, and mothers.

In Relational Discipleship (RD) mature disciple maker teams walk with each disciple and answer all questions at every level.

"You need milk, not solid food! Anyone who lives on milk, being still an infant, is not acquainted with the teaching about righteousness" (Hebrews 5:11–14). "I am writing to you, dear children … fathers … young men … Do not love the world or anything in the world" (1 John 2:12–15).

Chapter 4: Jesus Christ's Five Foundational Elementary Basics

Knowing Jesus Christ's five elementary teachings is essential to become more like Christ in everything you think, say and do. Mature Christ likeness is described as "the mature, who by constant use have trained themselves to distinguish good from evil" (Hebrews 5:14).

"Therefore let us go on and get past the elementary stage in the teachings *and* doctrine of Christ (the Messiah), advancing steadily toward the completeness *and* perfection that belong to spiritual maturity. Let us not again be laying the foundation of repentance *and* abandonment of dead works (dead formalism) and of the faith [by which you turned] to God, with teachings about purifying, the laying on of hands, the resurrection from the dead, and eternal judgment *and* punishment. [These are all matters of which you should have been fully aware long, long ago]" (Hebrews 6:1–2 AMP).

Please study carefully Jesus's teaching on each point.

Disciple Makers Must Emphasize These Foundational Kingdom Principles:

1. Religious stuff does not make me Christlike. Religion makes me feel good, but God requires me to actually be good, and attempting to be living like Jesus Christ at the moment of my death. To avoid the eternal lake of fire and gain eternal life with almighty God, I must stop all my man-made religious traditions and simply do what Jesus Christ did and commanded. (1 John 3:21–24, 4:17)
2. Jesus Christ taught who God is and how to have faith in God. My biblically qualified disciple maker will reveal God to me and teach me how to have faith in God. (John 17:6–8)
3. Jesus taught his disciples how to spiritually wash and pronounce God's forgiveness. I must regularly confess and repent of my sins to God and receive God's restoration-forgiveness, sometimes pronounced by New Covenant

members. (Matthew 15:18–22; John 13:6–17, 20:21–23; 1 John 1:8–10; Revelation 3:2–6, 22:14)
4. Jesus taught that every human being will be resurrected to face Creator God's judgment. My keeping the New Covenant terms provides me eternal life with God and escape from death with the devil in the lake of fire. (John 5:22–27)
5. Jesus taught that being in the New Covenant from almighty God and obeying the covenant terms (obeying Jesus teachings), provides eternal life with God and escape from the eternal dying experience of Satan the Devil and his victims. (John 5:25–29)

Jesus Christ taught these elementary facts as His essentials. We must believe them.

Chapter 5: Introduction to The Lifetime Terms of the New Covenant

(The full presentation is provided in Part 3.)

- I stay on God's soul rest path to hear Holy Spirit (Jeremiah 6:16; Matthew 11:29, 15, 13:9, 43).
- I add Christ's attitude and character traits to become Christlike (2 Peter 1:5–8).
- I obey Jesus Christ's commands (Matthew 5:19, 28:20).
- I trust Jesus Christ's promises (2 Peter 1:4).
- I spiritually wash regularly to remain useful for God (2 Timothy 2:21; John 13:14–17, 20:22–23; Galatians 6:1–2; Ephesians 2:10).

My continual practice of these produce my personal maturity (Hebrews 5:14).

Chapter 6: Relational Discipleship, the Teaching-Learning Model for Disciples of Jesus Christ

This instruction manual for making disciples of Jesus Christ began with a personal invitation to become our disciple. Many before you who considered us their wise spiritual parents or grandparents enjoyed the guilt-free learning experience that came from a peaceful, grace-filled home. From observing our daily examples of following Jesus Christ, they identified God's good and perfect will for their own peace-filled life in the midst of this world's chaos.

We repeated the relational discipleship model that Jesus Christ offered to the twelve apostles by getting close to one other through online connections, phone calls, and text messages.

If you are called by God to consider this book as a personal discipleship experience, you can learn our processes for maintaining a strong personal relationship with God as your heavenly Father. (John 6:37, 65)

While we can no longer welcome new disciples into our home, we offer you the foundation and formula for becoming and making disciples.

Jon Dean and Donna Smith

Chapter 7: Counting the Cost to Be Jesus Christ's Disciple

Did Jesus really mean that you must be willing to give up everything when He said, "Those of you who do not give up everything you have cannot be my disciples"? (Luke 14:25–34).

It's shocking to understand that Jesus Christ taught that many who try to be saved will not be able to be saved. "Someone asked him, "Lord, are only a few people going to be saved?" He said to them, "Make every effort to enter through the narrow door, because many, I tell you, will try to enter and will not be able to" (Luke 13:23–24).

It is also difficult to understand that Jesus Christ taught that most churches do not teach God's truth. He said, "Enter by the narrow gate; for wide is the gate and broad is the way that leads to destruction, and there are many who go in by it. Because narrow is the gate and difficult is the way which leads to life, and there are few who find it" (Matthew 7: 13–14).

The Cost of the Narrow Gate

In simple terms, I enter into The Narrow Gate whenever I realize that I need a personal Savior. I acknowledge that He offers me the New Covenant to get into the Kingdom of God. I beg almighty God to accept me into His spiritual family and save me from Satan and the hell that I am presently headed towards. Further, I ask for the gift of Faith to trust and obey everything within the Kingdom of God.

I beg God to accept Jesus Christ as my personal Savior and release within me the joy of His salvation. I ask the Lord Jesus Christ in heaven:

- to daily accept me,
- to daily save me and
- to daily affirm me to our heavenly Father.

The Cost of the Narrow Road

Daily denying one's own desires about everything, to learn and obey Jesus Christ's teachings through the Holy Spirit's power within, is keeping and staying within the New Covenant until earth life is over. These are two parts to this teaching, what God *offers* and what God *requires* to stay in covenant and in His favor. Today, God's covenant that came from Jesus Christ is the New Covenant. Just as Jesus taught it would be, most ministers fail to teach the New Covenant from Jesus.

In simple terms, the New Covenant is repenting of all of one's sins and accepting all that Jesus Christ did to become one's personal savior. Jesus said that only a few people will find the Narrow Road.

Since almighty God always offers a life contract/covenant to humans, one must know what God offers in today's New Covenant with Him and what terms God requires to maintain or remain in His contract/covenant.

Simply stated, the Bible answer from Jesus Christ is that Christians must:

(1) Be in Jesus Christ's New Covenant.

(2) Keep its terms (deny one's self and obey Jesus teachings on every subject) every day of earth life.

(3) Quickly confess and repent from every sin to heavenly Father (with a witness, if you can) each time one disobeys Jesus's teaching and receive God's immediate forgiveness and cleansing.

Bible Christianity can be described as living your earth life by obeying Jesus Christ's teaching about everything. Too many find it difficult to submit to almighty God's control on every life matter.

Jesus once reminded everyone about the importance of staying within God's love;

"If you keep my commands, you will remain in my love, just as I have kept my Father's commands and remain in his love. I have told you this so that my joy may be in you and that your joy may be complete." (John 15:10–11)

To each Christian in the New Covenant, almighty God says through Christ, the Mediator of a new covenant, that you will:

- Find your own soul rest
- Worship God in spirit and in truth.
- Be born again by the Holy Spirit.
- Receive His law in your mind and in your heart
- Be one of God's people
- Know God
- Be forgiven your wickedness and
- He will remember your sins no more.
- Receive a new heart of flesh, replacing one of stone
- Receive His Spirit within you
- Receive power to follow His decrees and keep His laws
- Become a daily New Covenant minister, who daily denies self and completes God's will as Jesus demonstrated, to receive the eternal rewards he deliberately laid up, while on earth.

(Luke 22:20; Matthew 11:28–30; John 3:3–8,14–18, 4:23–24; Hebrews 8:10–12, 9:15; Ezekiel 36:25–27; 2 Corinthians 1:22; Romans 8:14–16; 2 Corinthians 3:2–7; Luke 9:23; Matthew 6:19–21, 19:28–30; Luke 22:28–30)

Our Witness Testimonies

While reading our true stories and testimonies of God's full provision for us and our family through more than sixty years of trusting and obeying Him, you will learn how to enjoy the same benefits. We learned how to be content with much or with little in the same ways that Jesus's first-century leaders did. These stories appear in Chapter 8 and Part Five.

In *The Hidden Truth*, we welcome you to learn how we remain holy as God is holy. Peter commanded, "But just as He who called you is holy, so be holy in all you do; for it is written: "Be holy, because I am holy" (1 Peter 1:5–17).

You will learn how both Donna and I overcame our own sinful strongholds and assisted our disciples to "come to their senses and escape from the trap of the devil, who has taken them captive to do his will" (2 Timothy 2:22–26). We will show you how to correctly apply God's Word which enables you to remain holy. "I will put my Spirit within you so that you will obey my laws and do whatever I command" (Ezekiel 36:27 TLB).

We will show you how pure-hearted brothers and sisters assist one another to remain clean, useful vessels for our heavenly Father's use. It is a wonderful way to live (Matthew 18:15–22; John 13:8–17; 20:21–23; Romans 8:1–7; Galatians 6:1–10; James 5:16–20; 2 Timothy 2:20–26).

You will also learn to accept the great motivation offered by Jesus Christ to willingly pay your own cost. "Jesus replied, I assure you that when the world is made new and the Son of Man sits upon his glorious throne. Everyone who has given up houses or brothers or sisters or father or mother or children or property, for my sake, will receive a hundred times as much in return and will inherit eternal life" (Matthew 19:27–30 NLV).

In these pages, we openly share our personal motivations that inspire us to pay the daily cost to be effective disciples of Jesus Christ.

Chapter 8: A Life of Relational Discipleship

The first thing to know about us is that our life goal is to become as much like Jesus Christ as we can and to be living like Him at the moment of our last breath. Of course, we have not reached full maturity yet. However, after years of self-denial, obeying God's duty, and faithfully finishing God's tasks within our accountable discipleship, God has placed much of Jesus Christ's attitude within Donna and within me (Isaiah 53:10–12). For many years, we've systematically worked to develop Christ's attitude described in Philippians 2:2–18.

The second thing is that we both have transformed renewed minds that quickly identify God's good, pleasing, and perfect will. Our self-controlled daily application of God's ways produced many Christlike changes within us.

The third thing is that we know how to disciple others. Because we have worked on twelve church staffs, planted four churches and six state prison discipleships, and opened our home to many people, we tell you with confidence that Jesus Christ's disciple-making pattern works. Relational Discipleship (RD) has proven to be an effective repeatable model no matter where you live. More than fifty years of making disciples of Lord Jesus Christ brings us wonderful joy.

The close relationship that Jesus Christ had with each of His disciples resulted in their spiritual safety and maturity. In a similar way, God brought many into our home who completed RD with us and became excellent, successful Christlike citizens. Many of whom then offered the same personal RD to those God brought to them.

Over the years we used modern communication tools to make disciples for Jesus Christ. Many in RD with us enjoy regular informal visits through free Internet services. A small number of our disciples live nearby and are often in our home.

The Holy Spirit continues to affirm the truths you read in this book. Be greatly encouraged as you dig deeply into every portion of heavenly Father's revelation.

Relational Discipleship Fulfills the Great Commission

"Make disciples of all nations, baptizing them in the name of the Father, Son, and Holy Spirit, teaching them to obey everything I have commanded you. I am with you to the very end of the age" (Matthew 28:16–20).

Jesus guarantees His spiritual presence whenever disciples are made according to His instructions. Today through RD, we experience Jesus's presence as the Holy Spirit provides God's words of life and spirit. Because the Holy Spirit transformed us to have the same attitude as Jesus Christ, we daily live like Him in this world. This book is the way we can present Jesus Christ living through us to you. We demonstrate to you the same words (lessons) that Jesus demonstrated and taught to His first twelve apostles (John 17:6–8).

Entering into Relational Discipleship gives the disciple maker permission to hold you accountable as you learn and obey the same things that Jesus Christ taught His disciples to obey through accountability with Him. In Part Three you will find many of the same lessons that Jesus Christ taught.

Disciples Make Disciples

We believe that Jesus Christ requires His disciples to make other disciples. During His earthly ministry, Jesus Christ demonstrated God's concern for His family. Jesus and the apostles displayed how God wants His people cared for. We believe that the same way Jesus Christ made disciples should continue until the end of time (Matthew 28:19; John 15:1–17).

We believe that within the New Covenant, each one is obligated to daily become more like Jesus Christ and identify those whom God brings to them in order to duplicate the teacher-student process of Jesus Christ. RD is a personal display of real-life care from the disciple maker by which God opens the disciple's heart and mind for life changes.

Understand and Practice Relational Discipleship

No one cares how much you know until they know how much you care. The disciple maker and disciple agree to learn and obey everything that Jesus commanded while he or she expects Jesus's supernatural presence. Together they construct a plan (a yoke and burden) that works for them both. This is a personal agreement (covenant) by which the veteran Christ follower offers RD to his or her student.

This covenant (plan) covers subjects, availability, types of instruction, assignment formats, accountability, and beginning and ending dates. It fits each one's life schedule and does not overload either of them. Adjustments must be considered from either person's viewpoint and made with much sensitivity.

Disciple Makers: Patterns to Develop the Attitude of Jesus Christ

Your Disciple Maker (DM) remains open to growing more like Jesus Christ. If you believe that your DM team does or teaches anything that is not biblically sound or correct, they expect you to gracefully question them. Then, whenever biblical error or sin is confirmed, they will humbly and quickly confess and repent from the sin and receive gentle restoration, which you can provide. On the other hand, if no sins are discovered, gentle restoration is provided for that as well. RD results in the Disciple Maker and the Disciple both thinking more like Christ, living more like Christ, and achieving greater spiritual unity in God's Word. Both will more consistently apply the truths described in Philippians 2:2–18.

Consider the passages under each of the following topics.

Disciple Makers protect Disciples as Jesus did.

"I am the good shepherd; I know my sheep and my sheep know me—just as the Father knows me and I know the Father—and I lay down my life for the sheep" (John 10:14–15).

"While I was with them, I protected and kept them safe" (John 17:11–12).

"Follow Me, and I will make you fishers of men" (Matthew 4:19 KJV).

"… taught them many things by parables" (Mark 4:2).

Your Disciple Maker tests and questions you like Jesus did.

"He asked … to test him, for he already had in mind what he was going to do" (John 6:6).

"Why are you so afraid?" (Matthew 8:26).

"Why did you doubt?" (Matthew 14:31).

"Why are you talking among yourselves about having no bread?" (Matthew 16:8).

"Anyone who has seen me has seen the Father. How can you say, 'Show us the Father'?" (John 14:9).

Your Disciple Maker corrects you like Jesus did.

"I tell you, if you have faith as small as a mustard seed, you can say" (Matthew 17:20).

"'Teacher,' said John, 'we saw someone driving out demons in your name and we told him to stop, because he was not one of us.' 'Do not stop him,' Jesus said. 'For no one who does a miracle in my name can in the next moment say anything bad about me'" (Mark 9:38–39).

"Do not rejoice that the spirits submit to you, but rejoice that your names are written in heaven" (Luke 10:20).

"He rebuked Peter. 'Get behind me, Satan!' he said. 'You do not have in mind the concerns of God, but merely human concerns'" (Mark 8:33).

"He rebuked them for their lack of faith and their stubborn refusal to believe" (Mark 16:14).

"But He turned and rebuked them, and said, 'You do not know what kind of spirit you are of; for the Son of Man did not come to destroy men's lives, but to save them'" (Luke 9:55–56 NASB).

Your Disciple Maker expects you to verify the lessons.

"My teaching is not my own. It comes from the one who sent me. Anyone who chooses to do the will of God will find out whether my teaching comes from God or whether I speak on my own" (John 7:16–17).

"Anyone who loves me will obey my teaching ... Anyone who does not love me will not obey my teaching. These words you hear are not my own; they belong to the Father who sent me" (John 14:23–24).

Your Disciple Maker teaches about the Holy Spirit.

"Receive the Holy Spirit" (John 20:22).

"The Spirit of truth ... will be in you" (John 14:15–18).

"The Holy Spirit ... will teach you all things and will remind you" (John 14:26).

"The Spirit of truth ... will guide you into all the truth ... he will tell you what is yet to come" (John 16:13–15).

"True worshipers ... worship the Father in the Spirit and in truth, for they are the kind ... the Father seeks. God is spirit and his worshipers must worship in the Spirit and in truth" (John 4:23–24).

"Much more will your Father in heaven give the Holy Spirit to those who ask him" (Luke 11:13).

"Rivers of living water will flow from within them ... he meant the Spirit" (John 7:37–39).

Your Disciple Maker warns you like Jesus did.

If I continually disobey, Jesus will burn me like a weed (Matthew 3:12; Luke 3:17–18).

If I disown Jesus before men, He will disown me before the heavenly Father (Matthew 10:33; Mark 8:38).

If I do not produce kingdom fruit, I will end miserably (Matthew 8:12, 21:41–45; Mark 12:9; Luke 20:16).

If I find fulfillment in anything other than Christ, I will miss heaven (Matthew 10:39; Mark 8:35; Luke 9:24; John 12:25).

If I stop obeying and loving Jesus Christ, I will miss heaven (Matthew 10:37; Luke 14:26).

Your Disciple Maker will release you to make more disciples.

"Father, as you sent me into the world, I have sent them into the world" (John 17:1–18).

"Go and make disciples" (Matthew 28:19).

"Bear much fruit, showing yourselves to be my disciples. Everything that I learned I have made known to you. I chose you and appointed you [to] go and bear fruit that will last" (John 15:8, 13–16).

The Hidden Truth

Your Disciple Maker copies the ways of the apostles.

"Follow my example, as I follow the example of Christ" (1 Corinthians 11:1).

"I urge you to imitate me" (1 Corinthians 4:16).

"Join others in following my example according to the pattern we gave you" (Philippians 3:17 NIRV).

"Whatever you have learned or received or heard from me or seen in me—put it into practice. And the God of peace will be with you" (Philippians 4:9).

"You ought to follow our example, a model for you to imitate" (2 Thessalonians 3:7, 9).

"You became imitators of us and of the Lord and a model to believers" (1 Thessalonians 1:6–7).

Your Disciple Maker suggests a daily routine that includes:

- Daily soul rest start-up.
- Daily work on one of Jesus's promises.
- Daily work on one of Jesus's commands.
- Daily work on Christlike traits.
- Daily work on stopping all sins.
- Other items requiring accountability.

Suggested Relational Discipleship Covenant (Agreement)

On an agreed day, the Ds and DMs enter into a relational discipleship covenant. They affirm the expectations they have of one another and give one another permission to deal straightforward in sharing truth as best as they each understand it. They agree upon how the terms will be changed, should it become necessary. They will enjoy the peace and comfort that Jesus Christ provides them through the Holy Spirit by making disciples in the same way that He did.

Brief Summary of Relational Discipleship

Today's disciples submit to their disciple makers in order to learn the points that Jesus taught, namely:

- to identify the person or team that brings God's peace into their lives from God (Jesus for the twelve apostles)
- to enter into a disciple and disciple maker (RD) agreement (i.e., the Twelve taking Jesus's yoke and covenant)
- to learn to confess/repent from sin to God before a new covenant witness and accept gentle restoration (Galatians 6:1–10))
- to develop the attitude traits of Jesus Christ (use attitude-character traits lists)
- to learn to believe and trust in every promise of Jesus Christ (use the promise list)
- to learn to obey Jesus Christ's commands (use the command list),
- to daily apply one's own soul rest routines (i.e., Jeremiah's and Jesus's paths)
- to make other disciples in the same way, when one is trained and released.

Relational Discipleship Testimonies

The following testimonies were received from those Donna and I discipled over the years.

Testimony #1

Relational Discipleship (RD) is walking through this life with the help of a true brother and sister in Christ. It is a journey with a family that really loves you and wants the best God has to offer. It is learning how to be a disciple of Christ with people who are going through life ahead of you and who God has placed in your life to show you how they did it and how they are doing it. Our disciple maker team members (DM) are Christlike and God-loving people who want to see their Christian family know the actual way into the kingdom of heaven.

They are true shepherds of God's flock, which is under their care in all of life's situations. They have corrected us through gentle restoration as we have confessed our sins to one another. They have been humble and receptive to any advice or correction we have offered to them. They taught us a lot about the Bible and the love of Christ.

Our DM team really does want to do God's will in the short time we all have left on this earth. It is not playtime with them. Don't get me wrong. They enjoy life and friends, but they do not want to be playing church. They are serious about the kingdom of heaven and entering into covenant with God. It is a blessing to be in RD, walking in the new covenant of Jesus Christ. (Rudy & Janet P. Weatherford, TX)

Testimony #2

Entering into a relational discipleship covenant with my DM team was one of the best decisions I made in my life. They lovingly corrected wrong beliefs that I once had. They assisted me in properly choosing a husband. They supported me through financial gifts when I needed assistance as a student and as a newlywed. Overall, the experience was a huge blessing. My heart was ready to receive the correction they gave, and I am a stronger Christian woman because of it.

The outcomes of their discipleship including an increase of peace in my life, the ability to handle difficult situations using sound biblical practices, an understanding that I can only change my reactions to tough times and challenges, and that it is not up to me to change other people.

I also gained assurance of my place in heaven as well as understanding my role as a wife, sister, daughter, and future mother. I welcomed a wonderful and blessed marriage and a marriage partner who was also willing to be changed through the Holy Spirit-led relational discipleship of my DM team. I gained an understanding of the importance of daily cleansing my white robes so I can walk in the freedom from sin because Jesus died on the cross for me.

Jesus Christ said. "No one puts new wine into old wine skins; otherwise the wine will burst the skins, and the wine is lost and the skins as well; but one puts new wine into fresh wine skins." I knew that I did not want to be the old wineskin that Jesus could not put new wine into. I wanted to be moldable and pliable so that all the teachings of Jesus and His disciples could still be placed into my heart. My DM team were the people He used to help me learn Jesus's "new wine" teachings so that I could throw out the Pharisee-like teaching I had received previously through religion. (Merritt K., Arlington, TX)

Testimony #3

My journey within relational discipleship (RD) started with my marriage counseling. When my husband refused biblical processes and filed for divorce, my disciple maker team (DMT) walked with me during the separation and divorce. They always cared enough to share biblical perspectives about my life and relationships, which continuously strengthened my spiritual health. Each application of biblical truth in the midst of various difficult situations brought more peace and order to my life.

It was my privilege to live with my DMT for two years, observe many dynamics of a godly marriage, and receive countless applicable day-to-day teachings. The strong authority from their teachings came from their own daily obedience to the Lord, which I witnessed in many life situations. They demonstrated humility to receive advice as well as take ownership of their sins.

As we walked out life together, they encouraged me to develop my personal relationship with the Lord and the Holy Spirit. They consistently denied themselves to assist Holy Spirit to maximize whom God created me to become, strengthened in God's Word. I was encouraged and comforted without compromise to address and take ownership of difficult topics and gradually fill my heart with God's truth.

RD helped me learn how to apply biblical principles to my daily life. I learned about the Lord's forgiveness through spiritual foot washing and experienced true freedom from past strongholds and cravings of my flesh. Almighty God working through Holy Spirit-inspired RD has truly changed my life. God's principles will always be applicable because God's Word is the foundation of the kingdom of God.

I have obtained a great amount of personal peace and understanding of my eternal purposes. I now accept the fact that many people identify and appreciate spiritual fruit from biblical principles, but few will pay a price to apply them in their own lives. Within RD, we each continue to encourage both the seekers as well as those who are made ready by the Lord.

The Lord has now brought me several seekers who have watched my work lifestyle. They ask me for truth about real-life issues they face. Then, as they consistently receive God's truth from me (coming from Holy Spirit within my heart), they often seek to become serious friends. Some of them actually enter into close relationship with me and then continue the RD processes that I experienced.

My walk with the Lord is not without difficulties or mistakes, but the processes that I learned help me to overcome and not be a victim.

Among the great blessings of my life is watching a precious person with a troubled countenance become lighthearted and refreshed after receiving a portion of God's truth that they needed. I love to see their eyes and faces express real hope for their futures. When this happens (and it does quite often), it is as Jesus Christ said to Governor Pilate, "Everyone who is of the Truth [who is a friend of the Truth, who belongs to the Truth] hears and listens to my voice" (John 18:37 AB). I encourage everyone to pray that almighty God will identify his or her own disciple-making team. (Lena B., Ft. Worth, TX)

Testimony #4

Jesus called His disciples to come be with Him twenty-four hours a day, seven days a week, and three hundred sixty-five days a year for more than two years. Jesus was their teacher and He taught them everything the Father gave to Him. After Jesus's ascension, the disciples were to go and "make disciples of all nations, baptizing them in the name of the Father and of the Son and of the Holy Spirit, and teaching them to obey everything I have commanded you" (Matthew 28:19–20).

Today all Christians should do the same. My disciple maker helped me overcome an addiction that I could not handle by myself. It was embarrassing to obey Jesus's command and confess the same sin repeatedly to my disciple maker. Each time he gave me God's grace and assured me of our heavenly Father's forgiveness.

However, in reality, that is one of the points that helps anyone choose not to sin. I knew that if I did give in to the temptation and sin, I would have to confess. Therefore, with the strength of the Holy Spirit, I turned and walked away from the temptation.

In the 1940s, there was a popular song titled "I'll Walk Alone." I rejoice in the fact that in relational discipleship no one has to walk alone. Having one older in the faith guiding you, pronouncing God's forgiveness to you, correcting you, encouraging you, and loving you is worth more than silver or gold. It has been such a joy to see the change in people's lives as they submit to the process of biblical relational discipleship. Marriages have been resurrected. The lonely have shared their lives with others and changed occupations so that God-given talents are maximized.

Rather than singing "I'll Walk Alone," I am joyfully singing "I Walked Today Where Jesus Walked" along with my disciple maker. (Donna S, Ft. Worth, TX)

Testimony #5

I first met JD and Donna Smith through the avenue of patient care. At this point in my career, I had walked alongside thousands of people having lost or losing their mobility and struggling to find meaning and purpose in their remaining years. *Kind* and *peaceful* were the adjectives I would later use to describe my first exchange with them.

Years later, in the Spring of 2017, I found myself in darkness. I walked the aisle to accept Christ at a church camp in my younger years, rarely missed a Sunday morning church service, led worship music in the local church for almost a decade, and served as a deacon and an elder for another decade. Yet, I could no longer reconcile the inconsistencies of my daily life; the sin patterns that I blanketed with cheap grace, the anger lurking around each and every circumstance that did not go my way, the lack of purpose as a business owner, husband, and father, the mysterious depression that lingered after having found my way to the pinnacle of the American Dream, and ultimately the anxiety that led to the cardiac symptoms I had one evening. Instead of exhaling my final breath, when the Father allowed me to look to Him from the pit of my despair, I surrendered.

"Break me, make me, mold me into the man you want me to be" was my prayer. Tears flowed onto the keys of the family piano as I staggered through the words of a hymn I'd sang all my life: "All to Jesus... I surrender... all to You I freely give. "

Having a degree in "religious plasticity", I had nowhere to turn now but to the Holy Spirit Himself. *Lead me, guide me, direct me.* After a lengthy season of brokenness, the Father led me to JD

Smith. As JD and I began meeting for relational discipleship, I quickly discovered that my initial adjectives of kind and peaceful were not a religious facade. JD has since taught me how to posture myself to hear and walk with our heavenly Father through the gift of the Counselor. He has shown me that our Creator is using life's circumstances to Father me into maturity; not for my self-exaltation but rather for His glory and for His purposes. What a restful, peaceful place to be! I am forever thankful that our Father joined my earthly path to cross with JD and Donna Smith. If you are a surrendered believer, the truths found in this book will allow the Holy Spirit to transform you in ways beyond man's comprehension. (John R., Texas)

The Hidden Truth

A Preview of The Lifetime Terms of the New Covenant

It is wonderful to realize the true importance of what Jesus Christ taught the apostles in the light of God's New Covenant. Yes, we know that the apostles were commanded to teach each new disciple to obey what they learned from Jesus Christ to obey. And yes, we know that Jesus Christ's body and blood were accepted by almighty God as the sacrifice to establish the eternal New Covenant with humanity (Luke 22:18–20).

But most people do not realize that Jesus Christ's teachings are the terms to be kept of the eternal New Covenant of God's Kingdom, and that Jesus's teachings are the actual final exam for every human being (John 12:47–50). Seriously consider that the creator of the universe Himself offers you an eternal covenant for a deep personal relationship right now and forever. So, of course, you want to know what God expects from you and what He offers you; the terms of this eternal agreement, this New Covenant.

This information is explained through Jesus Christ's teachings. His words and life example describe what the Creator requires from you and what the Creator offers to you. In the same way that Israel's kings daily studied God's Covenant Terms, we need daily reviews of Christ's major teachings.

Here we list them as Five Terms of God's New Covenant.

The Five Terms

- Term One introduces the rest for your souls Jesus Christ offers in Matthew 11:29. You need soul rest before you can hear what God's Holy Spirit wants to tell you.
- Obeying Term Two develops Jesus Christ's attitude and character in you.
- Obeying Term Three keeps you doing what Jesus commands you to do to stay in Jesus's love (John 15:10–11).
- Obeying Term Four keeps you trusting/believing what God requires you to.

- Obeying Term Five keeps you forgiven, washed clean and useful to our heavenly Father.

"When he sits on the throne as king, he must copy for himself this body of instruction on a scroll in the presence of the Levitical priests. He must always keep that copy with him and read it daily as long as he lives. That way he will learn to fear the LORD his God by obeying all the terms of these instructions and decrees" (Deuteronomy 17:18–19 NLT).

Part Three: The Lifetime Terms of the New Covenant

The hidden truth is that Jesus Christ's New Covenant enables one to become enough like Christ to establish the Kingdom of God and the will of God on the earth.

Biblical Christianity is a lifestyle of supernaturally becoming transformed by the Holy Spirit into Christlikeness by deliberately choosing to obey the teachings of Jesus Christ (keeping the terms of the New Covenant). Therefore, the most important thing in one's life is knowing and obeying the terms of the New Covenant.

Jesus Christ taught what God requires of a person in Covenant with Him. The blessings of God offered in the New Covenant are also described in detail by Jesus Christ. Please join us in looking at these teachings as terms of the New Covenant, established by Jesus's death. Please consider that Jesus Christ was actually introducing his New Covenant terms when he showed the differences with the more familiar terms of Moses's Old Covenant. "You have heard that it was said, But I tell you…" (Matthew 5:21–22, 27–28). Also, when the scribes and Pharisees attempted to catch Jesus in breaking Old Testament law, I believe that His responses were demonstrations of the New Covenant of the kingdom of God.

Finally, at the last supper, Jesus used the term New Covenant. "In the same way, after the supper he took the cup, saying, "This cup is the new covenant in my blood, which is poured out for you" (Luke 22:20). This New Covenant Prayer is both an introduction of almighty God's kingdom ways and His will.

New Covenant Terms are presented as if you were writing them down for yourself. Read or speak them from your heart.

My New Covenant Prayer

"Heavenly Father, thank you for creating everything and establishing Your New Covenant through Jesus Christ of Nazareth, the King of your kingdom.

High Priest-Jesus Christ in heaven, thank you for obeying heavenly Father to become his New Covenant sacrifice for me. Please become my Savior and Door into the kingdom of God.

Holy Spirit within me, please continue to purify, empower and fill my heart with God's truth and Christlike love. I am desperate for you to counsel and guide me every moment of my life.

Father, thank you for my disciple maker who is revealing You to me as I learn to obey everything that Jesus commanded His apostles to obey. I will become and remain Holy as you are, Father.

I officially now enter your everlasting New Covenant. Through its inward spiritual provisions and outward relational discipleship processes, I promise to keep myself a clean, useful vessel for You. When released by my disciple maker, I will make disciples of those precious persons that you draw to me.

Amen."

Chapter 9 – New Covenant Term One

I Stay on God's Soul Rest Path to Hear Holy Spirit

"Take my yoke upon you and learn from me, for I am gentle and humble in heart, and you will find rest for your souls" (Matthew 11:29).

Term One introduces the "rest for your souls" offered by Jesus. Why do I need soul rest? To hear what God's Holy Spirit wants to tell me, I use Step 1 to control my soul, my spirit, my heart and my body. This practice develops my spiritual ear to consistently hear the Holy Spirit.

To introduce the biblical concept of walking in Soul Rest, we need the truth that Lord Jesus gave, that almighty God is a spirit and not a human. In John 4:23–26, we learn that almighty God seeks worshippers who know how to worship Him in spirit and in truth. We know that God has always had steady communication with certain ones of His spiritual family.

It's been a great revelation to understand, practice, and teach the ancient paths of soul rest spoken of by Jeremiah and King David. The ten steps presented here will help you find the personal soul rest Jesus Christ offered His disciples. His Holy Spirit is placed within each New Covenant member for this very purpose; to enable almighty God to regularly fellowship with each one in God's family. (Ezekiel 36:25–27; Romans 8:16)

For Christ followers who want to worship God in spirit and in truth, we have listed ten proven, helpful steps from the Bible, stated in modern words to strengthen regular, daily fellowship between Holy Spirit and God's family.

My Daily Ten Step Morning Spiritual Routine

Step 1: Report to God for My Spiritual Warfare Duty

Say aloud, "In Jesus Christ's name, I offer my body as a living sacrifice, holy and pleasing to you, almighty God, as my spiritual act of worship. I will be Your righteous servant and slave all night and day, enabled by Holy Spirit to keep the terms of Your New Covenant" (Adaptations from Romans 12:1–3, 6:13, 19).

Say aloud, "Our Father in heaven, hallowed be Your name, Your kingdom come, Your will be done, on earth as it is in heaven. Give us today our daily bread. And forgive us our debts, as we also have forgiven our debtors. And lead us not into temptation, but deliver us from the evil one. For yours is the kingdom and the power and the glory forever, Amen" (Matthew 6:6–13).

When needed, I use as many of the remaining nine steps as necessary to remain a victorious worker for almighty God.

Step 2: Enter into God's Ancient Soul Rest Path

I Quiet My Soul

Say aloud, "In Jesus Christ's name, my soul, you be balanced and operate just like Jesus Christ's own soul. My thoughts, I take you captive. You center upon God's truth about every subject. My willpower, you choose God's ways all day, directed by God's peace. My emotions/feelings, you stop flooding over me unrighteously. Function like Jesus Christ's feelings and emotions did." (Adaptations of Psalms 62:1, 5. 116:7; 131:1–2; Isaiah 26:3; 2 Corinthians 10:5)

I Control My Spirit

Say aloud, "In Jesus Christ's name, my spirit, you be active and alert all day and night. Reject every evil thing and communicate only with the Holy Spirit, God's angels, and righteous human spirits. Reveal to my mind the information that the Holy Spirit and you collect. My spirit, function as God created you to." (Adaptations of

Ezekiel 36:26; 1 Corinthians 14:32; Romans 8:16; Proverbs 25:28; 20:27; Matthew 26:41; John 4:23–24)

I Control My Heart

Say aloud, "In Jesus Christ's name, my heart, be pure and holy. Honor almighty God with your outflow all day and night. Welcome the Holy Spirit all night and day. What is in you will always come out, so do not take in any unrighteous, evil, selfish, sinful thoughts, images, words, or deeds. My heart, be on guard all day and night." (Adaptations of Ezekiel 36:24–27; Proverbs 4:20–23)

I Control My Body

Say aloud, "In Jesus Christ's name, my body, I direct you to function correctly just like the body of Jesus Christ. Welcome only the Holy Spirit and God's angels and resist every other spirit. You be pure, holy, balanced, and separate from all worldliness. Do not crave, demand, or accept anyone's or my worship. Be ready to be replaced by my victorious spiritual body whenever God says it is time to be with Him." (Adaptations of 1 Thessalonians 4:3–8; 1 Corinthians 6:1–20, 7:1; Philippians 3:18–19)

Step 3: Ask, Seek and Knock

Say aloud, "In Jesus Christ's name, heavenly Father, today please give me everything I need. Reveal all you want me to know and open every door of opportunity to advance your kingdom truth wherever I am." (Adaptations of Matthew 7:7–8)

Step 4: Secure My Calling and Election into God's Family

Say aloud, "In Jesus Christ's name, I put into my life Jesus Christ's traits of goodness, knowledge, self-control, perseverance, godliness, brotherly kindness, and agape love. Becoming more like Jesus Christ causes me to be more effective and productive for You, dear Father." (Adaptations of 2 Peter 1:3–11)

Step 5: Offer This Clean Heart Prayer

Say aloud, "In Jesus Christ's name, dear Father, I will confess my sins to You in front of a brother or sister when I can. But right now, please purify my heart and strengthen Your Holy Spirit's fellowship with my spirit. Enable me to speak and live in such kingdom truth that people around me will ask serious questions of me." (Adaptations of Psalm 51:10–13)

Step 6: Apply Jesus's Beatitudes

Say aloud, "In Jesus Christ' name, I am spiritually penniless, Father. Help me. My spiritual blindness is so dark. Give me understanding. I fear directing my own life. Please give me more Holy Spirit self-control and meekness. I am starving and thirsting for a deeper relationship with You, Father. Please make me kindhearted as Jesus is and place Your calmness and peace wherever I am. Thank You for strengthening me to endure whatever suffering You ask of me to advance Your kingdom today. I look forward to enjoying the rewards You have awaiting my obedience." (Adaptations of Matthew 5:3–12; Numbers 12:3)

Step 7: Welcome the Holy Spirit's Ministry

Say aloud, "In Jesus Christ's name, Father, please pour more of the Holy Spirit's anointing within my heart now. Overflow like fresh spiritual spring water through my thoughts, words, and deeds to continue Jesus Christ's ministry. Enable me to finish each of Your tasks and receive Your 'Well done' and the Holy Spirit's blessings." (Adaptations of Luke 11:13; John 7:38–39; Isaiah 11:2–3; Galatians 4:6; Romans 8:13; Galatians 5:16–18, 25)

Step 8: Apply God's Spiritual Authorizations

Say aloud, "In Jesus Christ's name, I exercise my authority to preach the kingdom of God at home and work without using religious words that offend anyone. By applying God's truth to every situation today, I exercise my authority to overcome every evil hindrance or obstacle. The consistent, amazing, and excellent quality of my service and production will draw questioners to me to develop relationships. Father, please reveal which persons I need to offer Your truth to that will lead them to their deliverance, healing, or good news of the kingdom of God." (Adaptations of Luke 9:1–2, 10:17–20; Mark 16:19–20)

Step 9: Resist the Enemy

Say aloud, "In Jesus Christ's name, heavenly Father, I am totally submitted to You right now. Please provide a full guard on me all night and day from Your Holy Spirit and Your angels that You assign to me. To remain effective for You, Father, I will stay in truth, be righteous in everything, spread/maintain peace, recall Your faithfulness, think and speak Your words of truth, and always pray about everything."

"Satan and demons listen to me. almighty God owns me. King Jesus Christ has given me His authority to use His name. Nothing you do will spiritually harm me or separate me from the love of almighty God."

"In Jesus Christ's name, I resist you all night and day. The Lord God Himself rebukes you! I flatten and squash all your evil agents. I will not listen to or receive anything your agents attempt to put in my thoughts or heart. You cannot force upon me any dreams, visions, fears, illnesses, infirmities, mountainous obstacles, or gigantic hindrances."

"In Jesus Christ's name, get out of my life right now." (Adaptations of James 4:7; 1 Peter 5:8–9; Matthew 18:10; Psalm 91:11; Hebrews 1:14; Acts 12:11; Ephesians 6:10–18; Luke 10:19; 2 Timothy 2:25–26)

Step 10: I Promise Obedience to God's New Covenant

Say aloud, "In Jesus Christ's name, heavenly Father, **I will** obey Your every command, trust and stand on Your every promise, add Jesus Christ's attitude and character traits to myself, overcome every enemy temptation, spiritually wash away my every sin in the blood of the Lamb of God (Jesus Christ), and welcome your supernatural power from Holy Spirit, residing within my new heart."

"By walking in your narrow New Covenant path, and keeping my soul at rest, ***I will not*** drift away from You, harden my heart to Your messages, fall away from You, deliberately sin against You, and I will not turn away from You."

"I am confirming my calling and election by doing Your will with great delight, because I want to move into my residence that Lord Jesus has prepared in your heavenly city. Thank you so much for everything, heavenly Father. Amen." (Adaptations of: Matthew 5:17–20, 7:14, 11:29, 26:41; 2 Peter 1:3–11; John 13:13–17, 14:1-3; Ezekiel 36:25–27; Jeremiah 6:16; Hebrews 2:1–4, 3:6–4:14, 6:4–8, 10:26–31, 11:16, 12:25–29; 1 Corinthians 15:1–2; Revelation 21:1–27)

Chapter 10– New Covenant Term Two

I Add Christ's Attitude and Character Traits to Become Christlike

Obeying Term Two is Jesus's process of developing His own likeness within me. One powerful result of learning how to become like Jesus Christ and obey His teachings where I live is the tremendous spiritual effect on others.

When obedient New Covenant members daily live this way, their service to Jesus Christ is both pleasing to God and approved by men (Romans 14:17). At the same time, this one's daily life wins the respect of outsiders (1Thessalonians 5:11–12), and supernaturally draws precious people to us.

First, we study the details of the very attitude of Jesus Christ as the Apostles taught it (Philippians 2:2–18). I want that attitude of Jesus. Toward that achievement, I will perform the following:

- always serve others
- assist others to accomplish their interests
- become blameless and pure
- be positive instead of negative
- deny self to build relationships
- do everything without arguing or grumbling
- do nothing out of selfish ambition or vain conceit
- easily accept my role as student or teacher
- expect to receive God's "well done"
- hold firmly to God's words of truth
- honor all authorities
- humble myself
- make myself nothing
- manage my own interests correctly
- pour out my life for my family and neighbors
- overcome every sin through the steps in 2 Timothy 2:21–26
- value all others above myself

- work out my salvation with fear and trembling as the Holy Spirit within me accomplishes God's purposes

Secondly, we carefully observe the required Christlike character traits of the mature Christians who were placed in charge of local churches. From the Apostles teachings (1 Timothy 3:1–13; Titus 1:5–9) we identified 180 brief descriptions of Christlike maturity. The goal of each New Covenant member is to move closer to the standard Jesus established. Please also see 2 Peter 1:3–11.

God wants every son and daughter of His to daily become more like Jesus Christ. We have discovered that being like Jesus is what supernaturally draws precious people to us. Our students and disciples tell us that the following list is one of the most powerful and popular teaching tools they've considered.

180 Characteristics of Jesus Christ

When I stand before Jesus, I want Him to say these things about me. Adaptations from Timothy 3:1–13; Titus 1:5–9; 1 Peter 1:1–11.

1. I am marked by honesty and integrity in my approach to life.

2. I am trustworthy and demonstrate it naturally.

3. I earn respect by my conduct.

4. I do not have a greedy desire for the approval of others.

5. I am well thought of and have a good reputation among people in general.

6. I am unaware of anything that anyone could use as an accusation against me.

7. I have forgiven all who have offended me.

8. I do not know of any broken relationships in my life that I have ignored.

9. When I discover that I have offended someone, I atone immediately, desiring to be godly and a righteous person.

10. I am not flirtatious with anyone.

11. I am not mentally or physically promiscuous.

12. If married, I am committed to meeting the needs of my marriage partner.

13. If married, I enjoy my spouse's company.

14. If married, I speak tenderly and gently to my spouse.

15. If married, I develop and maintain an atmosphere of encouragement and acceptance through continual affirmation.

16. If married, I love my spouse deeply and express that love in every possible way.

17. If married, my marriage exhibits the grace of God.

18. If married, I have one spouse of the opposite sex.

19. I am not promiscuous or overly attracted to anyone.

20. My physical and mental life is pure.

21. I am not carried away to extremes.

22. My life is marked by balance and stability.

23. I am not influenced by praise.

24. I am not crushed by criticism.

25. I am not carried away by my successes, power, title, or position.

26. I am even tempered.

27. I am not volatile.

28. I am easily renewed and refueled for ministry.

29. I am a well-balanced and well-adjusted person.

30. I am not flighty or constantly jumping from one thing to another.

31. I am not an overly nervous person.

32. I do not overdo anything in my life.

33. My response to most of life's situations would be considered peaceful by others.

34. I am a prudent, wise, and thoughtful person.

35. My personal judgment enables me to identify the harmful effects of extremes.

36. The basis of my decision-making process is humility, God's grace, and a desire to manage well what God has given to me.

37. I recognize that my position is secondary to God's authority.

38. I try to make God look good and never overly focus on myself.

39. I show good judgment in life.

40. I do not take myself too seriously and hold my abilities in proper perspective.

41. Reasonable, balanced people see me as a humble person.

42. I have self-control.

43. God's inward peace manages my life.

44. I conduct all that I do in an honorable way.

45. People show respect for me.

46. I have a well-ordered life.

47. My life and character attract others to truth and then to Christ.

48. I am perceived as being pleasant.

49. My life decorates the gospel and does not detract from it.

50. My orderly life reflects that God is a God of order.

51. Others find my company a joy and a blessing.

52. I am aware of what is going on around me and meet the needs of God's family.

53. I am not overly moved by life's events and circumstances.

54. I am a caretaker of God's resources to serve others, just as if I was serving Jesus.

55. I administer the possessions given to me by God in a way that reflects the character of God—food, drink, housing, clothing, care of the sick, and visits to those in institutions.

56. I use my home for others, showing God's love and freedom from the love of possessing.

57. I understand that earthly possessions are temporary and spiritual possessions are eternal.

58. I have a teachable spirit, modeling God's truth in a humble and sensitive way.

59. I am not quarrelsome.

60. I am kind, patient, and gentle when I am correcting those in opposition to me.

61. I am secure in Christ and secure in myself by daily keeping God's new covenant terms.

62. I am in control of my personality (mind, will, and emotions).

63. I love and live by God's Word and help others understand the freedom of its principles.

64. Others say that I am an encourager.

65. When I teach God's Word, I show an aptitude for handling Scripture with care and reasonable skill.

66. I have a good understanding of the essential, foundational truths of God's Word.

67. I am able to communicate Scripture to others in such a way that they see God and not me.

68. I recognize false biblical teachings and offer firm but gentle ways to correct its misuse.

69. I am not addicted to chemicals like alcohol or drugs of any kind.

70. I have learned to control my body and appetites.

71. I am not driven by overindulgence into improper behavior.

72. I do not exhibit any behavior that would cause my brother or sister in Christ to stumble.

73. If I drink alcoholic beverages, it is in moderation, to avoid causing another to stumble.

74. I understand that my body is not my own and is the residence of the Holy Spirit of God.

75. I am not violent.

76. I never express meanness in the form of physical, verbal, emotional, or spiritual abuse.

77. I deal wisely with offenses that might otherwise result in abuse.

78. I am in control of my own spirit, soul, and body.

79. I do not criticize or attack persons, families, businesses, or ministries verbally or physically in any way.

80. I do not engage in gossip or defame another person's character.

81. Others regard me as mild-mannered, meek, and patient.

82. People are relaxed in my presence.

83. I listen more than I speak.

84. I am able to resolve problems without losing control of my emotions.

85. I am not viewed as being overly authoritative.

86. I never retaliate when wronged.

87. I hold such a high view of others that I never abuse or take advantage of people.

88. I am solutions oriented rather than problem oriented.

89. I do not insist on my rights.

90. I do not do or say anything that would destroy unity.

91. I am a peacemaker.

92. I am more interested in achieving harmony than forcing my own way.

93. I am not threatened by competition.

94. I am willing to bend and compromise when necessary without breaking biblical principles.

95. I lead with a servant's heart.

96. I am not stubborn, insisting on my own point of view at all costs.

97. I am not argumentative.

98. A spirit of competition does not drive me.

99. I am free from the love of money.

100. I seek God's kingdom first.

101. I am not devastated by the loss of things.

102. I have learned to be content in every circumstance.

103. My happiness is not the result of material possessions.

104. I am not allured by money, nor is it a status symbol.

105. I have achieved a balance between excessive frugality and excessive spending.

106. I do not find my security in money.

107. I fully believe that God is my provider.

108. I do not measure people's worth by their material possessions, but I look to their hearts.

109. I believe my employment is a gift from God.

110. I am not lazy but enjoy honest work opportunities in a wide variety of duties.

111. I believe I am to be a good manager of God's resources.

112. My lifestyle is simple.

113. I am not attracted to get-rich-quick schemes.

114. I have no problem disclosing my finances with more spiritually mature believers.

115. Others recognize me as a giver.

116. I manage my family well.

117. All members of my family have a mutual respect and love for one another.

118. My home is an expression of God's love and peace.

119. I understand that each family member has their own will to choose my values or not.

120. My home is a place where life lessons are learned and big decisions are made in the context of love.

121. I understand that my children's experience with me determines their view of God.

122. I have taught my children to be obedient and courteous in their responses.

123. I do not avoid family problems but lovingly and gently address all family concerns.

124. I do not run from problems nor refuse to face them.

125. I am progressing in becoming more like Lord Jesus Christ.

126. I have been tested and proven morally and ethically through my life and the handling of relationships.

127. I know that learning and applying biblical principles and heavenly wisdom takes time.

128. I understand that some believers mature more quickly than others do.

129. I do not depend upon my strength to bring forth success.

130. I do not control others to get my way.

131. I do not manipulate, intimidate, or dominate others in any way.

132. I do not count upon my personality, education, finances, magnetism, or intelligence to achieve what God wants.

133. I fully believe and practice "that which is highly esteemed among men is an abomination in the sight of God," as Jesus described in Luke 16:15.

134. I have learned that God works with people of humble and contrite hearts.

135. I am a servant to all.

136. I have a good reputation with outsiders and within my community.

137. My neighbors, coworkers, and acquaintances who may not agree with my spiritual convictions still respect me as a person.

138. I am not overbearing, domineering, or controlling.

139. I am not self-willed, and I easily submit to legitimate authorities in my life.

140. I am recognized as a team player.

141. I readily admit when I am wrong.

142. I am more oriented toward others than myself.

143. I practice an honest goodness rather than a pretentious self-righteousness.

144. I do not have to continually validate or justify myself in the eyes of others.

145. I am not stubborn or arrogant.

146. Others find it easy to discuss their opinion with me and seek my counsel because they realize I attempt to be impartial and fair.

147. I understand that anger can never achieve the righteousness of God.

148. I am not quick-tempered.

149. I am not easily threatened.

150. I am not quick to retaliate.

151. I do not hold grudges against others and do not have a bitter spirit toward any person.

152. I choose not to be offended when I am wronged.

153. I do not have sudden outbursts of anger when something does not go my way.

154. I do not earn my living by producing, distributing, or selling anything that violates God's Word, character, or will, and I do not break any laws of the land.

155. I am neither fond of nor involved in any wrongful practices that could result in a fraudulent gain.

156. I love what is considered good by God's Word and standards.

157. I love the beauty of what God has made and what He has done.

158. I enjoy His creation and am in awe of His New Covenant plan of salvation.

159. I focus every day on what is good.

160. I love the things that honor God.

161. I hate what God hates.

162. I am known as being fair in my dealings with people and am always concerned that others perceive me as fair.

163. I am concerned about giving a fair day's work for a fair day's pay.

164. I am capable of making wise judgments.

165. I attempt to go through life with a moment-by-moment awareness of the presence of God.

166. My life is marked by a love for God that embraces each activity in life through kingdom lenses.

167. I try to be sensitive to sin and avoid all unholy behavior.

168. I believe it is possible to be in the world without being a part of the world.

169. I carefully abstain from anything that could cause harm to my body, mind, or spirit.

170. By the Holy Spirit, I receive more love, joy, peace, patience, kindness, goodness, faithfulness, gentleness, and self-control.

171. I hold firmly to the faith.

172. I understand, hold to, and attempt to conserve God's truth.

173. I encourage others while I refute those who oppose the truth.

174. Because I know God's love, I express that love to others.

175. My commitment is to the Great Commandment and the Great Commission.

176. I know that the pattern for protection and the spread of the gospel is to make disciples.

177. I am submitted to discipleship of others.

178. I am making disciples who obey what Jesus commanded until Christ is fully formed in them.

179. I am upright and honest.

180. I am holy and sanctified.

Chapter 11– New Covenant Terms Three and Four

I Obey Jesus Christ's Commands and Trust His Promises

As we introduce the promises and commands that Jesus taught his apostles, consider how they prepare you for your own eternal final exam. This teaching is almighty God's Eternal Final Exam preparation.

"If anyone hears my words but does not keep them, I do not judge that person. For I did not come to judge the world, but to save the world. There is a judge for the one who rejects me and does not accept my words; the very words I have spoken will condemn them at the last day" (John 12:47–48).

Please pause a moment to consider the enormous treasure before you. As best we can identify them, what follows is every commandment and every promise given by Jesus Christ. These are the central truths that Jesus Christ taught the founders of our faith. See how important Jesus says obeying His commands are in John 15:10 and Matthew 5:19, and the importance of Jesus's promises described in 2 Peter 1:3–4.

Imagine the changes you will experience as the Holy Spirit begins to write each command and promise on your heart. See how Paul describes this in 2 Corinthians 3:2–6. Knowing the kingdom of God commands, and the promised treasures and rewards awaiting as a result of obedience, completely changed my life and those of many friends.

This chapter may become one of the most significant studies you have ever undertaken. As Jesus said, these words from the heavenly Father are the actual judgment factors by which your life will be evaluated. May God bless you richly as He increases your deep understanding of these significant words expressly provided to humanity.

It is such a privilege to provide Jesus Christ's commands and promises for you. Please enjoy learning what is so important to heavenly Father.

A quick review:

Obeying Term Three keeps me doing what Jesus commands me to do, to stay in His love (John 15:10–11).

Obeying Term Four keeps me trusting/believing what God requires me to.

Jesus Christ's Promises and Commands

About God's commands, Jesus said: "Therefore anyone who sets aside one of the least of these commands and teaches others accordingly will be called least in the kingdom of heaven, but whoever practices and teaches these commands will be called great in the kingdom of heaven" (Matthew 5:19). "Therefore go and make disciples of all nations, baptizing them in the name of the Father and of the Son and of the Holy Spirit, and teaching them to obey everything I have commanded you. And surely I am with you always, to the very end of the age" (Matthew 28:19–20).

About God's promises, the Apostle Peter said: "His divine power has given us everything we need for a godly life through our knowledge of him who called us by his own glory and goodness. Through these he has given us his very great and precious promises, so that through them you may participate in the divine nature, having escaped the corruption in the world caused by evil desires" (2 Peter 1:4).

Lesson 1: Promise of Eternal Life for Believers who Daily Obey Christ

- They will not be driven away. "Then Jesus declared, 'I am the bread of life. He who comes to me will never go hungry, and he who believes in me will never be thirsty. But as I told you, you have seen me and still you do not believe. All that

the Father gives me will come to me, and whoever comes to me I will never drive away'" (John 6:35–37).
- They shall not perish. "Just as Moses lifted up the snake in the desert, so the Son of Man must be lifted up, that everyone who believes in him may have eternal life. For God so loved the world that he gave his one and only Son, that whoever believes in him shall not perish but have eternal life" (John 3:14–16).
- He has crossed from death to life. "I tell you the truth; whoever hears my word and believes him who sent me has eternal life and will not be condemned; he has crossed over from death to life" (John 5:24).
- They will be raised at the last day. "For my Father's will is that everyone who looks to the Son and believes in him shall have eternal life, and I will raise him up at the last day" (John 6:40).
- He has everlasting life. "I tell you the truth; he who believes has everlasting life" (John 6:40).
- They will never die. "Jesus said to her, 'I am the resurrection and the life. He who believes in me will live, even though he dies; and whoever lives and believes in me will never die. Do you believe this?'" (John 11:25–26).
- They will be saved. "Whoever believes and is baptized will be saved, but whoever does not believe will be condemned" (Mark 16:16).

Lesson 2: Command to Daily Live a Repentant Life

- Repent, or Jesus will remove my Holy Spirit fellowship. "From that time on Jesus began to preach, 'Repent, for the kingdom of heaven is near'" (Matthew 4:17). "Remember the height from which you have fallen! Repent and do the things you did at first. If you do not repent, I will come to you and remove your lampstand from its place" (Revelation 2:5).
- Each day I must first find and obey His kingdom ways in order to receive from Him. "But seek first his kingdom and his righteousness, and all these things will be given to you as well" (Matthew 6:33).

- Each day I must ask, seek, and knock. "Ask and it will be given to you; seek and you will find; knock and the door will be opened to you" (Matthew 7:7).
- Each day I must come to Christ to receive my soul rest "Come to me, all you who are weary and burdened, and I will give you rest" (Matthew 11:28).
- Daily following Him requires denying my own way and doing His way (which I hate doing). "Then Jesus said to his disciples, 'If anyone would come after me, he must deny himself and take up his cross and follow me'" (Matthew 16:24).
- I give forgiveness to others to receive my own forgiveness "And when you stand praying, if you hold anything against anyone, forgive him, so that your Father in heaven may forgive you your sins" (Mark 11:25).
- My daily obedience to His commands opens heaven's narrow door for me. "He said to them, 'Make every effort to enter through the narrow door, because many, I tell you, will try to enter and will not be able to'" (Luke 13:24).

Lesson 3: Promise of the Father's Gift of the Holy Spirit

- There's a gift for those who ask. "If you then, though you are evil, know how to give good gifts to your children, how much more will your Father in heaven give the Holy Spirit to those who ask him" (Luke 11:13).
- Eternal life is at the well. "But whoever drinks the water I give them will never thirst. Indeed, the water I give them will become in them a spring of water welling up to eternal life" (John 4:14).
- Living water flows from within. "On the last and greatest day of the festival, Jesus stood and said in a loud voice, 'Let anyone who is thirsty come to me and drink. Whoever believes in me, as Scripture has said, rivers of living water will flow from within them.' By this, he meant the Spirit, whom those who believed in him were later to receive. Up to that time the Spirit had not been given, since Jesus had not yet been glorified" (John 7:37–39).

- The true Spirit Counselor is with us forever. "And I will ask the Father, and he will give you another advocate to help you and be with you forever—the Spirit of truth. The world cannot accept him, because it neither sees him nor knows him. But you know him, for he lives with you and will be in you" (John 14:16–17).
- There's an offer of breath and the Holy Spirit. "And with that he breathed on them and said, "Receive the Holy Spirit" (John 20:22).
- The promised clothing of power is available. "I am going to send you what my Father has promised; but stay in the city until you have been clothed with power from on high" (Luke 24:49).
- Baptism with the Holy Spirit is possible. "But you will receive power when the Holy Spirit comes on you; and you will be my witnesses in Jerusalem, and in all Judea and Samaria, and to the ends of the earth" (Acts 1:8).

Lesson 4: Command to Be Christ's Witness in the Holy Spirit's Power

- Receive the Holy Spirit. "And with that he breathed on them and said, 'Receive the Holy Spirit'" (John 20:22).
- Let God's children first be filled. "First let the children eat all they want," he told her, "for it is not right to take the children's bread and toss it to the dogs" (Mark 7:27).
- To drink, one must be thirsty. "On the last and greatest day of the festival, Jesus stood and said in a loud voice, "Let anyone who is thirsty come to me and drink. Whoever believes in me, as Scripture has said, rivers of living water will flow from within them" (John 7:37–38).
- Obeying prepares the way to receive the Counselor. "If you love me, keep my commands. And I will ask the Father, and he will give you another advocate to help you and be with you forever—the Spirit of truth. The world cannot accept him, because it neither sees him nor knows him. But you know him, for he lives with you and will be in you" (John 14:15–17).

- Ask in His name and receive full joy. "Until now you have not asked for anything in my name. Ask and you will receive, and your joy will be complete" (John 16:24).
- We must be empowered to witness. "I am going to send you what my Father has promised; but stay in the city until you have been clothed with power from on high" (Luke 24:49).
- We must testify of Christ as the Holy Spirit does. "When the Advocate comes, whom I will send to you from the Father—the Spirit of truth who goes out from the Father—he will testify about me. And you also must testify, for you have been with me from the beginning" (John 15:26–27).

Lesson 5: Promise of the Holy Spirit's Activity

- He convicts of sin, righteousness, and guilt in judgment. "When he comes, he will prove the world to be in the wrong about sin and righteousness and judgment" (John 16:8).
- He spiritually births like the wind blows. "The wind blows wherever it pleases. You hear its sound, but you cannot tell where it comes from or where it is going. So it is with everyone born of the Spirit" (John 3:8).
- He gives life. "The Spirit gives life; the flesh counts for nothing. The words I have spoken to you—they are full of the Spirit and life" (John 6:63).
- He testifies about Christ. "When the Advocate comes, whom I will send to you from the Father—the Spirit of truth who goes out from the Father—he will testify about me" (John 15:26).
- He teaches and reminds of Christ's words. "But the Advocate, the Holy Spirit, whom the Father will send in my name, will teach you all things and will remind you of everything I have said to you" (John 14:26).
- He gives guidance and advance notice. "But when he, the Spirit of truth, comes, he will guide you into all the truth. He will not speak on his own; he will speak only what he hears, and he will tell you what is yet to come" (John 16:13).
- To the receivers, He gives power to witness. "But you will receive power when the Holy Spirit comes on you; and you

will be my witnesses in Jerusalem, and in all Judea and Samaria, and to the ends of the earth" (Acts 1:8).

Lesson 6: Command to Share the Gospel

- Share the gospel (good news). "As you go, proclaim this message: 'The kingdom of heaven has come near ... He said to them, "Go into all the world and preach the gospel to all creation" (Matthew 10:7; Mark 16:15).
- Freely give. "Heal the sick, raise the dead, and cleanse those who have leprosy, drive out demons. Freely you have received; freely give" (Matthew 10:8).
- Call all into discipleship. "Therefore go and make disciples of all nations, baptizing them in the name of the Father and of the Son and of the Holy Spirit" (Matthew 28:19).
- Teach them to obey. "And teaching them to obey everything I have commanded you. And surely I am with you always, to the very end of the age" (Matthew 28:20).
- Bring into the open whatever is concealed. "For whatever is hidden is meant to be disclosed, and whatever is concealed is meant to be brought out into the open" (Mark 4:22).
- Begin where you are. "He told them, 'This is what is written: The Messiah will suffer and rise from the dead on the third day, and repentance for the forgiveness of sins will be preached in his name to all nations, beginning at Jerusalem'" (Luke 24:46–47).

Three Levels of Sharing

1. Spiritual babies need special care, "feed my lambs".
2. Accountable relational discipleship, "take care of my sheep".
3. Lifetime provision of Spirit-Life-Words, "feed my sheep".

"When they had finished eating, Jesus said to Simon Peter, 'Simon son of John, do you love me more than these?' 'Yes, Lord,' he said, 'you know that I love you.' Jesus said, 'Feed my lambs.' Again, Jesus said, 'Simon son of John, do you love me?' He answered, 'Yes, Lord, you know that I love you.' Jesus said, 'Take care of my sheep.' The third time he said to him, 'Simon son of John, do you love me?'

Peter was hurt because Jesus asked him the third time, 'Do you love me?' He said, 'Lord, you know all things; you know that I love you.' Jesus said, 'Feed my sheep'" (John 21:15–17).

Lesson 7: Promise of Power to Overcome Satan's Activities

- Spiritual harm is prevented by exercising Christ's authority. "He replied, 'I saw Satan fall like lightning from heaven. I have given you authority to trample on snakes and scorpions and to overcome all the power of the enemy; nothing will harm you'" (Luke 10:18–19).
- Leaders govern the church family. "Truly I tell you, whatever you bind on earth will be bound in heaven, and whatever you loose on earth will be loosed in heaven" (Matthew 18:18).
- At times, believers drive out demons in Christ's name. "And these signs will accompany those who believe: In my name they will drive out demons; they will speak in new tongues" (Mark 16:17).
- At times, believers fast and pray. "However, this kind does not go out except by prayer and fasting" (Matthew 17:21).
- Satan has been judged and defeated at Calvary. "Now is the time for judgment on this world; now the prince of this world will be driven out" (John 12:31).
- Christ frees completely. "So if the Son sets you free, you will be free indeed" (John 8:36).
- Illnesses placed by Satan should be removed by God's power "Then should not this woman, a daughter of Abraham, whom Satan has kept bound for eighteen long years, be set free on the Sabbath day from what bound her?" (Luke 13:16).

Lesson 8: Command to Grow into Mature Love

- Suffer now to win later. "But I tell you, do not resist an evil person. If anyone slaps you on the right cheek, turn to them the other cheek also. And if anyone wants to sue you and take your shirt, hand over your coat as well. If anyone forces you to go one mile, go with them two miles" (Matthew 5:39–41).

- His love in us is our weapon. "But I tell you, love your enemies and pray for those who persecute you ... 'Put your sword back in its place,' Jesus said to him, 'for all who draw the sword will die by the sword'" (Matthew 5:44, 26:52).
- Become like our Father. "Be perfect, therefore, as your heavenly Father is perfect" (Matthew 5:48).
- How to become mature. "Jesus answered, 'If you want to be perfect, go, sell your possessions and give to the poor, and you will have treasure in heaven. Then come, follow me'" (Matthew 19:21). "Do not be afraid, little flock, for your Father has been pleased to give you the kingdom. Sell your possessions and give to the poor. Provide purses for yourselves that will not wear out, a treasure in heaven that will never fail, where no thief comes near and no moth destroys" (Luke 12:32–33).
- Love, do good, bless, and pray. "But to you who are listening I say: Love your enemies, do good to those who hate you, bless those who curse you, pray for those who mistreat you" (Luke 6:27–28).
- Lend without expectation. "But love your enemies, do good to them, and lend to them without expecting to get anything back. Then your reward will be great, and you will be children of the Most High, because he is kind to the ungrateful and wicked" (Luke 6:35).
- Stand firm now to gain later. "Stand firm, and you will win life" (Luke 21:19).

Lesson 9: Promise of God's Supernatural Protection

- Jesus calls His own into a close relationship. "I am the good shepherd; I know my sheep and my sheep know me" (John 10:14).
- No one can snatch God's family from Jesus's hand. "I give them eternal life, and they shall never perish; no one will snatch them out of my hand" (John 10:28).
- No one can snatch God's family from the heavenly Father's hand. "My Father, who has given them to me, is greater than

all; no one can snatch them out of my Father's hand" (John 10:29).
- Jesus keeps His own and raises them from death. "And this is the will of him who sent me, that I shall lose none of all those he has given me, but raise them up at the last day" (John 6:39).
- Through His name, Jesus protects. "While I was with them, I protected them and kept them safe by that name you gave me. None has been lost except the one doomed to destruction so that Scripture would be fulfilled" (John 17:12).
- End-time protection is provided. "If the Lord had not cut short those days, no one would survive. But for the sake of the elect, whom he has chosen, he has shortened them" (Mark 13:20).
- Angelic protection is offered. "See that you do not despise one of these little ones. For I tell you that their angels in heaven always see the face of my Father in heaven" (Matthew 18:10).

Lesson 10: Command to Be Salt and Light

- Do good deeds daily. "In the same way, let your light shine before others, that they may see your good deeds and glorify your Father in heaven" (Matthew 5:16).
- Minister first to your own family. "Jesus did not let him, but said, "Go home to your own people and tell them how much the Lord has done for you, and how he has had mercy on you" (Mark 5:19).
- Give God's mercy to others. "Be merciful, just as your Father is merciful" (Luke 6:36).
- I check my own spiritual guidance. "See to it, then, that the light within you is not darkness" (Luke 11:35).
- See the lost souls around you now. "Don't you have a saying, 'It's still four months until harvest'? I tell you, open your eyes and look at the fields! They are ripe for harvest" (John 4:35).
- Serve Him now. "Then Jesus told them, 'You are going to have the light just a little while longer. Walk while you have

the light, before darkness overtakes you. Whoever walks in the dark does not know where they are going'" (John 12:35).
- Fruit bearers get prayer results. "This is to my Father's glory, that you bear much fruit, showing yourselves to be my disciples ... You did not choose me, but I chose you and appointed you so that you might go and bear fruit—fruit that will last—and so that whatever you ask in my name the Father will give you" (John 15:8, 16).

Lesson 11: Promise when Mistreated for Living and Speaking like Christ

- Great heavenly rewards await. "Blessed are those who are persecuted because of righteousness, for theirs is the kingdom of heaven. Blessed are you when people insult you, persecute you and falsely say all kinds of evil against you because of me. Rejoice and be glad, because great is your reward in heaven, for in the same way they persecuted the prophets who were before you" (Matthew 5:10–12).
- The faithful will be saved. "You will be hated by everyone because of me, but the one who stands firm to the end will be saved" (Matthew 10:22).
- Not a spiritual hair on the head of the faithful will perish. "You will be betrayed even by parents, brothers and sisters, relatives and friends, and they will put some of you to death. Everyone will hate you because of me. But not a hair of your head will perish. Stand firm, and you will win life" (Luke 21:16–19).
- Words and wisdom can be received when needed. "But before all this, they will seize you and persecute you. They will hand you over to synagogues and put you in prison, and you will be brought before kings and governors, and all on account of my name. And so you will bear testimony to me. But make up your mind not to worry beforehand how you will defend yourselves. For I will give you words and wisdom that none of your adversaries will be able to resist or contradict" (Luke 21:12–15).

- Jesus acknowledges His own in heaven to our Father. "Whoever acknowledges me before others, I will also acknowledge before my Father in heaven" (Matthew 10:32).
- Jesus acknowledges His own before God's angels. "I tell you, whoever publicly acknowledges me before others, the Son of Man will also acknowledge before the angels of God" (Luke 12:8).
- When one is hated, excluded, insulted, and rejected, he is blessed. "Blessed are you when people hate you, when they exclude you and insult you and reject your name as evil, because of the Son of Man" (Luke 6:22).

Lesson 12: Command to Totally Love God

- Don't foolishly test God. "Jesus answered him, 'It is also written: "Do not put the Lord your God to the test"'" (Matthew 4:7).
- Worship and serve only the Lord God. "Jesus said to him, 'Away from me, Satan! For it is written: "Worship the Lord your God, and serve him only"'" (Matthew 4:10).
- Call no man on earth *father*. "And do not call anyone on earth 'father,' for you have one Father, and he is in heaven" (Matthew 23:9).
- Love the Lord God totally. "Love the Lord your God with all your heart and with all your soul and with all your mind and with all your strength" (Mark 12:30).
- Fear almighty God. "But I will show you whom you should fear: Fear him who, after your body has been killed, has authority to throw you into hell. Yes, I tell you, fear him" (Luke 12:5).
- Worship the Father in Spirit and in truth. "Yet a time is coming and has now come when the true worshipers will worship the Father in the Spirit and in truth, for they are the kind of worshipers the Father seeks" (John 4:23).
- Honor Jesus, and you honor our Father. "Moreover, the Father judges no one, but has entrusted all judgment to the Son, that all may honor the Son just as they honor the Father.

Whoever does not honor the Son does not honor the Father, who sent him" (John 5:22–23).

Lesson 13: Promise of Jesus's Many Comings

- When we obey His commission, Jesus is with us. "And teaching them to obey everything I have commanded you. And surely I am with you always, to the very end of the age" (Matthew 28:20).
- Jesus joins those gathered in His name. "For where two or three gather in my name, there am I with them" (Matthew 18:20).
- Jesus comes to us. We are not orphans. "I will not leave you as orphans; I will come to you" (John 14:18).
- Jesus, our Father, and His family are unified. "On that day you will realize that I am in my Father, and you are in me, and I am in you" (John 14:20).
- Jesus goes away and returns to us. "You heard me say, 'I am going away and I am coming back to you.' If you loved me, you would be glad that I am going to the Father, for the Father is greater than I" (John 14:28).
- Jesus show Himself to the obedient. "Whoever has my commands and keeps them is the one who loves me. The one who loves me will be loved by my Father, and I too will love them and show myself to them" (John 14:21).
- Jesus and our Father closely abide with the obedient. "Jesus replied, 'Anyone who loves me will obey my teaching. My Father will love them, and we will come to them and make our home with them'" (John 14:23).

Lesson 14: Command to Take Christ's Message Seriously

- Repent and believe His good news. "The time has come," he said. "The kingdom of God has come near. Repent and believe the good news" (Mark 1:15).
- Believe ahead of time that you have received. "Therefore I tell you, whatever you ask for in prayer, believe that you have received it, and it will be yours" (Mark 11:24).

- Trust Jesus, whom God sent to you. "Jesus answered, 'The work of God is this: to believe in the one he has sent'" (John 6:29).
- Believe Christ because of His work. "Do not believe me unless I do the works of my Father. But if I do them, even though you do not believe me, believe the works that you may know and understand that the Father is in me, and I in the Father" (John 10:37–38).
- Trust in Christ in order to become God's family. "Believe in the light while you have the light, so that you may become children of light." When he had finished speaking, Jesus left and hid himself from them" (John 12:36).
- Do not be troubled. Trust God and Jesus. "Do not let your hearts be troubled. You believe in God; believe also in me" (John 14:1).
- Believe that Jesus and the Father are unified. "Believe me when I say that I am in the Father and the Father is in me; or at least believe on the evidence of the works themselves" (John 14:11).

Lesson 15: Promise for the Humble, Lowly, Kind, and Pure Hearted

- The kingdom of heaven is received by the poor in Spirit. "Blessed are the poor in spirit, for theirs is the kingdom of heaven" (Matthew 5:3).
- God's comfort is received by the mourners. "Blessed are those who mourn, for they will be comforted" (Matthew 5:4).
- The earth is inherited by the meek. "Blessed are the meek, for they will inherit the earth" (Matthew 5:5).
- The hungry are filled with righteousness. "Blessed are those who hunger and thirst for righteousness, for they will be filled" (Matthew 5:6).
- Mercies will be shown to the merciful. "Blessed are the merciful, for they will be shown mercy" (Matthew 5:7).
- The sons of God are those who make peace. "Blessed are the peacemakers, for they will be called children of God" (Matthew 5:9).

- Those who see God are the pure in heart. "Blessed are the pure in heart, for they will see God" (Matthew 5:8).

Lesson 16: Command to Be a Humble Servant

- Take His yoke to find your soul rest. "Take my yoke upon you and learn from me, for I am gentle and humble in heart, and you will find rest for your souls" (Matthew 11:29).
- Serve instead of exercising authority. "Jesus called them together and said, "You know that the rulers of the Gentiles lord it over them, and their high officials exercise authority over them. Not so with you. Instead, whoever wants to become great among you must be your servant" (Matthew 20:25–26).
- Call your servant leaders brother or sister. "But you are not to be called 'Rabbi,' for you have one Teacher, and you are all brothers" (Matthew 23:8).
- A slave of all serves everyone. "Not so with you. Instead, whoever wants to become great among you must be your servant, and whoever wants to be first must be slave of all" (Mark 10:43–44).
- Rejoice at being in God's family, not at your ministry. "However, do not rejoice that the spirits submit to you, but rejoice that your names are written in heaven" (Luke 10:20).
- When honored, sit in the lowest place. "When someone invites you to a wedding feast, do not take the place of honor, for a person more distinguished than you may have been invited. If so, the host who invited both of you will come and say to you 'Give this person your seat.' Then, humiliated, you will have to take the least important place. But when you are invited, take the lowest place, so that when your host comes, he will say to you, 'Friend, move up to a better place.' Then you will be honored in the presence of all the other guests. For all those who exalt themselves will be humbled, and those who humble themselves will be exalted" (Luke 14:8–11).
- Accept no praise. Simply do your duty. "So you also, when you have done everything you were told to do, should say,

'We are unworthy servants; we have only done our duty'" (Luke 17:10).

Lesson 17: Promise for Obeying Jesus's Commands

- The great in God's kingdom practice and teach commands. "Therefore anyone who sets aside one of the least of these commands and teaches others accordingly will be called least in the kingdom of heaven, but whoever practices and teaches these commands will be called great in the kingdom of heaven" (Matthew 5:19).
- He will build His house wisely. "Therefore everyone who hears these words of mine and puts them into practice is like a wise man who built his house on the rock. The rain came down, the streams rose, and the winds blew and beat against that house; yet it did not fall, because it had its foundation on the rock" (Matthew 7:24–25).
- He will be loved by Jesus and our heavenly Father. "Whoever has my commands and keeps them is the one who loves me. The one who loves me will be loved by my Father, and I too will love them and show myself to them" (John 14:21).
- The obedient abides with our Father and Jesus. "Anyone who loves me will obey my teaching. My Father will love them, and we will come to them and make our home with them" (John 14:23).
- The obedient remain in Jesus's love. "If you keep my commands, you will remain in my love, just as I have kept my Father's commands and remain in his love" (John 15:10).
- They will be a friend to Jesus. "You are my friends if you do what I command" (John 15:14).
- They will enter into the new heavenly city to enjoy the Tree of Life. "Blessed are those who wash their robes that they may have the right to the tree of life and may go through the gates into the city" (Revelation 22:14).

Lesson 18: Command to Remain in Christ's Word

- Recognize false prophets (ministers). "Watch out for false prophets. They come to you in sheep's clothing, but inwardly they are ferocious wolves. By their fruit you will recognize them. Do people pick grapes from thorn bushes, or figs from thistles? Likewise, every good tree bears good fruit, but a bad tree bears bad fruit" (Matthew 7:15–17).
- Recognize yeast (false teachings and doctrines). "'Be careful,' Jesus said to them. 'Be on your guard against the yeast of the Pharisees and Sadducees'" (Matthew 16:6).
- Evaluate carefully what you hear. "'Consider carefully what you hear,' he continued. 'With the measure you use, it will be measured to you—and even more'" (Mark 4:24).
- Determine to retain what you hear. "Therefore consider carefully how you listen. Whoever has will be given more; whoever does not have, even what they think they have will be taken from them" (Luke 8:18).
- Especially appreciate Christ's Word. "Listen carefully to what I am about to tell you: The Son of Man is going to be delivered into the hands of men" (Luke 9:44).
- Diligently study Scripture about Christ. "You study the Scriptures diligently because you think that in them you have eternal life. These are the very Scriptures that testify about me" (John 5:39).
- Expect others to treat you like Christ was treated. "Remember what I told you: 'A servant is not greater than his master.' If they persecuted me, they will persecute you also. If they obeyed my teaching, they will obey yours also" (John 15:20).

Lesson 19: Promise for Following Jesus's Pattern

- They will have the light of life. "When Jesus spoke again to the people, he said, 'I am the light of the world. Whoever follows me will never walk in darkness, but will have the light of life'" (John 8:12).

- They will be given eternal life. "My sheep listen to my voice; I know them, and they follow me. I give them eternal life, and they shall never perish; no one will snatch them out of my hand" (John 10:27–28).
- They will find their own lives. "Then Jesus said to his disciples, 'Whoever wants to be my disciple must deny themselves and take up their cross and follow me. For whoever wants to save their life will lose it, but whoever loses their life for me will find it'" (Matthew 16:24–25).
- They will gain heavenly treasure. "Jesus answered, 'If you want to be perfect, go, sell your possessions and give to the poor, and you will have treasure in heaven. Then come, follow me'" (Matthew 19:21).
- They will have one hundred times more now. "Then Peter spoke up, 'We have left everything to follow you!' 'Truly I tell you,' Jesus replied, 'no one who has left home or brothers or sisters or mother or father or children or fields for me and the gospel will fail to receive a hundred times as much in this present age: homes, brothers, sisters, mothers, children and fields—along with persecutions—and in the age to come eternal life'" (Mark 10:28–30).
- They will become fishers of men. "'Come, follow me,' Jesus said, 'and I will send you out to fish for people'" (Matthew 4:19).
- They will be honored by our heavenly Father. "Whoever serves me must follow me; and where I am, my servant also will be. My Father will honor the one who serves me" (John 12:26).

Lesson 20: Command to Daily Live Like Christ

- Fulfill all righteousness and obey all His commands. "Therefore go and make disciples of all nations, baptizing them in the name of the Father and of the Son and of the Holy Spirit, and teaching them to obey everything I have commanded you. And surely I am with you always, to the very end of the age" (Matthew 28:19–20).

- Become gentle and humble in heart through Christ's yoke. "Take my yoke upon you and learn from me, for I am gentle and humble in heart, and you will find rest for your souls" (Matthew 11:29).
- Deny self. Take the cross daily. Follow Christ. "Then he said to them all: 'Whoever wants to be my disciple must deny themselves and take up their cross daily and follow me'" (Luke 9:23).
- Remember how Christ lived and died. "After taking the cup, he gave thanks and said, 'Take this and divide it among you. For I tell you I will not drink again from the fruit of the vine until the kingdom of God comes.' And he took bread, gave thanks and broke it, and gave it to them, saying, 'This is my body given for you; do this in remembrance of me'" (Luke 22:17–19).
- Father honors those who live like Jesus. "Whoever serves me must follow me; and where I am, my servant also will be. My Father will honor the one who serves me" (John 12:26).
- Do as Christ did. "Now that I, your Lord and Teacher, have washed your feet, you also should wash one another's feet. I have set you an example that you should do as I have done for you" (John 13:14–15).
- Love others with His love that is in you. "As the Father has loved me, so have I loved you. Now remain in my love" (John 15:9).

Lesson 21: Promise of Prayer Results

- He who asks, seeks, and knocks will receive. "For everyone who asks receives; the one who seeks finds; and to the one who knocks, the door will be opened" (Matthew 7:8).
- Our Father gives good gifts to those who ask. "If you, then, though you are evil, know how to give good gifts to your children, how much more will your Father in heaven give good gifts to those who ask him" (Matthew 7:11).
- If you believe, you will receive. "If you believe, you will receive whatever you ask for in prayer" (Matthew 21:22).

- Unity in God's will brings His results. "Again, truly I tell you that if two of you on earth agree about anything they ask for, it will be done for them by my Father in heaven" (Matthew 18:19).
- Results come from boldness. "I tell you, even though he will not get up and give you the bread because of friendship, yet because of your shameless audacity he will surely get up and give you as much as you need" (Luke 11:8).
- Results come for those who continue to pray. "And will not God bring about justice for his chosen ones, who cry out to him day and night? Will he keep putting them off? I tell you, he will see that they get justice, and quickly. However, when the Son of Man comes, will he find faith on the earth?" (Luke 18:7–8).
- Continual obedience to Jesus's words brings results. "If you remain in me and my words remain in you, ask whatever you wish, and it will be done for you" (John 15:7).

Lesson 22: Command for Faithfulness in Prayer

- Secret prayer in Jesus's name brings our Father's rewards. "Until now you have not asked for anything in my name. Ask and you will receive, and your joy will be complete" (John 16:24).
- Father knows, so don't jabber "And when you pray, do not keep on babbling like pagans, for they think they will be heard because of their many words. Do not be like them, for your Father knows what you need before you ask him" (Matthew 6:7–8).
- Follow Christ's example in prayer. "This, then, is how you should pray: 'Our Father in heaven, hallowed be your name, your kingdom come, your will be done, on earth as it is in heaven. Give us today our daily bread. And forgive us our debts, as we also have forgiven our debtors. And lead us not into temptation, but deliver us from the evil one'" (Matthew 6:9–13).

- Pray for those who mistreat and bless those who curse you "Bless those who curse you, pray for those who mistreat you" (Luke 6:28).
- Pray for more workers to be sent out. "He told them, 'The harvest is plentiful, but the workers are few. Ask the Lord of the harvest, therefore, to send out workers into his harvest field'" (Luke 10:2).
- To escape and stand always watch and pray. "Be always on the watch, and pray that you may be able to escape all that is about to happen, and that you may be able to stand before the Son of Man" (Luke 21:36).
- Remain alert to pray to prevent your personal sin. "'Why are you sleeping?' he asked them. 'Get up and pray so that you will not fall into temptation'" (Luke 22:46).

Lesson 23: Promise for the Use of Jesus's Name

- Bring glory to the heavenly Father. Ask in Jesus's name. "And I will do whatever you ask in my name, so that the Father may be glorified in the Son" (John 14:13).
- Always ask in Jesus's name. "You may ask me for anything in my name, and I will do it" (John 14:14).
- Produce lasting fruit by asking in Jesus's name. "You did not choose me, but I chose you and appointed you so that you might go and bear fruit—fruit that will last—and so that whatever you ask in my name the Father will give you" (John 15:16).
- When approved, Father gives. "In that day you will no longer ask me anything. Very truly, I tell you, my Father will give you whatever you ask in my name" (John 16:23).
- To receive complete joy, ask in Jesus's name. "Until now you have not asked for anything in my name. Ask and you will receive, and your joy will be complete" (John 16:24).
- In that day you will ask Father in Jesus's name. "In that day you will ask in my name. I am not saying that I will ask the Father on your behalf. No, the Father himself loves you because you have loved me and have believed that I came from God" (John 16:26–27).

- In Jesus's name, these signs will accompany believers. "And these signs will accompany those who believe: In my name they will drive out demons; they will speak in new tongues; they will pick up snakes with their hands; and when they drink deadly poison, it will not hurt them at all; they will place their hands on sick people, and they will get well" (Mark 16:17–18).

Lesson 24: Command to Earn Heavenly Treasures

- Give and loan. "Give to the one who asks you, and do not turn away from the one who wants to borrow from you" (Matthew 5:42).
- Store up heavenly treasure, not earthly treasure. "Do not store up for yourselves treasures on earth, where moths and vermin destroy, and where thieves break in and steal. But store up for yourselves treasures in heaven, where moths and vermin do not destroy, and where thieves do not break in and steal" (Matthew 6:19–20).
- Practice tithing, justice, mercy, and faithfulness. "Woe to you, teachers of the law and Pharisees, you hypocrites! You give a tenth of your spices—mint, dill and cumin. But you have neglected the more important matters of the law—justice, mercy and faithfulness. You should have practiced the latter, without neglecting the former" (Matthew 23:23).
- Give to the poor and become clean. "But now as for what is inside you—be generous to the poor, and everything will be clean for you" (Luke 11:41).
- Guard yourselves against all kinds of greed. "Then he said to them, 'Watch out! Be on your guard against all kinds of greed; life does not consist in an abundance of possessions'" (Luke 12:15).
- Invite the troubled to expect heavenly rewards. "Then Jesus said to his host, 'When you give a luncheon or dinner, do not invite your friends, your brothers or sisters, your relatives, or your rich neighbors; if you do, they may invite you back and so you will be repaid. But when you give a banquet,

invite the poor, the crippled, the lame, and the blind'" (Luke 14:12–13).
- Use wealth to gain eternal friendships. "I tell you, use worldly wealth to gain friends for yourselves, so that when it is gone, you will be welcomed into eternal dwellings" (Luke 16:9).

Lesson 25: Promise of Being Raised from the Dead

- The payday of the righteous is at the resurrection. "But when you give a banquet, invite the poor, the crippled, the lame, the blind, and you will be blessed. Although they cannot repay you, you will be repaid at the resurrection of the righteous" (Luke 14:13–14).
- God's children can no longer die. "But those who are considered worthy of taking part in the age to come and in the resurrection from the dead will neither marry nor be given in marriage, and they can no longer die; for they are like the angels. They are God's children, since they are children of the resurrection" (Luke 20:35–36).
- All are alive unto God. "But in the account of the burning bush, even Moses showed that the dead rise, for he calls the Lord 'the God of Abraham, and the God of Isaac, and the God of Jacob.' He is not the God of the dead, but of the living, for to him all are alive" (Luke 20:37–38).
- Jesus raises the dead just as the heavenly Father does. "For just as the Father raises the dead and gives them life, even so the Son gives life to whom he is pleased to give it" (John 5:21).
- At Jesus's voice all will be raised. "Do not be amazed at this, for a time is coming when all who are in their graves will hear his voice and come out—those who have done what is good will rise to live, and those who have done what is evil will rise to be condemned" (John 5:28–29).
- Jesus will raise His believers to eternal life at the last day. "For my Father's will is that everyone who looks to the Son and believes in him shall have eternal life, and I will raise them up at the last day" (John 6:40).

- Whoever believes in Jesus will never die. "Jesus said to her, 'I am the resurrection and the life. The one who believes in me will live, even though they die; and whoever lives by believing in me will never die. Do you believe this?'" (John 11:25–26).

Lesson 26: Command to Remain in Christ

- Make your personal tree good to receive good fruit. "Make a tree good and its fruit will be good, or make a tree bad and its fruit will be bad, for a tree is recognized by its fruit" (Matthew 12:33).
- First clean up the spiritually blind. "Pharisee! First clean the inside of the cup and dish, and then the outside also will be clean" (Matthew 23:26).
- Be positively different yet do not offend. "Salt is good, but if it loses its saltiness, how can you make it salty again? Have salt among yourselves, and be at peace with each other" (Mark 9:50).
- Rejoice and keep your name in heaven. "However, do not rejoice that the spirits submit to you, but rejoice that your names are written in heaven" (Luke 10:20).
- Spiritual birth is essential. "You should not be surprised at my saying, 'You must be born again'" (John 3:7).
- Work for food that lasts eternally. "Do not work for food that spoils, but for food that endures to eternal life, which the Son of Man will give you. For on him God the Father has placed his seal of approval" (John 6:27).
- To produce spiritual fruit, continue to obey Christ. "Remain in me, as I also remain in you. No branch can bear fruit by itself; it must remain in the vine. Neither can you bear fruit unless you remain in me" (John 15:4).

Lesson 27: Promise of Christ's Worldwide Coming

- Jesus comes with power and great glory. "At that time they will see the Son of Man coming in a cloud with power and great glory. When these things begin to take place, stand up

and lift up your heads, because your redemption is drawing near" (Luke 21:27–28).
- Jesus's coming will be as visible as lightning. "For as lightning that comes from the east is visible even in the west, so will be the coming of the Son of Man" (Matthew 24:27).
- His angels will gather His elect from the ends of heaven. "And he will send his angels with a loud trumpet call, and they will gather his elect from the four winds, from one end of the heavens to the other" (Matthew 24:31).
- Jesus comes to take His own to be with Him. "And if I go and make a place for you, I will come back and take you to be with me that you also may be where I am" (John 14:3).
- His ready and watchful servants will be waited upon by Jesus. "It will be good for those servants whose master finds them watching when he comes. Truly I tell you, he will dress himself to serve, will have them recline at the table and will come and wait on them. It will be good for those servants whose master finds them ready, even if he comes in the middle of the night or toward daybreak" (Luke 12:37–38).
- The faithful and wise servant will be in charge of Jesus's assets. "It will be good for that servant whom the master finds doing so when he returns. Truly I tell you, he will put him in charge of all his possessions" (Luke 12:43–44).
- Jesus will judge from His glorious heavenly throne. "When the Son of Man comes in his glory, and all the angels with him, he will sit on his glorious throne" (Matthew 25:31).

Lesson 28: Command to Be Ready for Christ's Coming

- Expect and watch for many deceivers. "Jesus said to them: 'Watch out that no one deceives you. Many will come in my name, claiming, 'I am he,' and will deceive many'" (Mark 13:5–6).
- Watch for Christ's sudden coming. "Therefore keep watch because you do not know when the owner of the house will come back—whether in the evening, or at midnight, or when the rooster crows, or at dawn. If he comes suddenly,

do not let him find you sleeping. What I say to you, I say to everyone: 'Watch!'" (Mark 13:35–37).
- Be ready for Christ's return. "Be dressed ready for service and keep your lamps burning, like servants waiting for their master to return from a wedding banquet, so that when he comes and knocks they can immediately open the door for him" (Luke 12:35–36).
- You never know when Christ will check on you. "You also must be ready, because the Son of Man will come at an hour when you do not expect him" (Luke 12:40).
- Do not treasure anything of this earth. "On that day no one who is on the housetop, with possessions inside, should go down to get them. Likewise, no one in the field should go back for anything. Remember Lot's wife" (Luke 17:31–32).
- Watch and guard your heart and feelings to be ready for His coming. "Be careful, or your hearts will be weighed down with carousing, drunkenness and the anxieties of life, and that day will close on you suddenly like a trap" (Luke 21:34).
- Hold on, wake up, make strong, and finish His assignments "Except to hold on to what you have until I come … Wake up! Strengthen what remains and is about to die, for I have found your deeds unfinished in the sight of my God. Remember, therefore, what you have received and heard; hold it fast, and repent. But if you do not wake up, I will come like a thief, and you will not know at what time I will come to you" (Revelation 2:25, 3:2–3).

Lesson 29: Promise for All Who Eat the Living Bread

- Jesus, the heavenly bread, gives life to the world. "For the bread of God is the bread that comes down from heaven and gives life to the world" (John 6:33).
- Jesus provides eternal food and drink. "Then Jesus declared, 'I am the bread of life. Whoever comes to me will never go hungry, and whoever believes in me will never be thirsty'" (John 6:35).

- He who eats will not die. "But here is the bread that comes down from heaven, which anyone may eat and not die" (John 6:50).
- The one who eats will live forever. "I am the living bread that came down from heaven. Whoever eats this bread will live forever. This bread is my flesh, which I will give for the life of the world" (John 6:51).
- The one who eats receives eternal life and resurrection. "Whoever eats my flesh and drinks my blood has eternal life, and I will raise them up at the last day" (John 6:54).
- The one who eats and drinks remains in Jesus. "Whoever eats my flesh and drinks my blood remains in me, and I in them" (John 6:56).
- Because of feeding on Jesus, one lives. "Just as the living Father sent me and I live because of the Father, so the one who feeds on me will live because of me" (John 6:57).

Lesson 30: Command to Live Wisely

- Evaluate peoples' characters before you share His wisdom. "Do not give dogs what is sacred; do not throw your pearls to pigs. If you do, they may trample them under their feet, and turn and tear you to pieces" (Matthew 7:6).
- Combine shrewdness and innocence. "I am sending you out like sheep among wolves. Therefore, be as shrewd as snakes and as innocent as doves" (Matthew 10:16).
- Be on guard against mankind. "Be on your guard; you will be handed over to the local councils and be flogged in the synagogues" (Matthew 10:17).
- Let heavenly Father remove the bad leaders. "He replied, 'Every plant that my heavenly Father has not planted will be pulled up by the roots. Leave them; they are blind guides. If the blind lead the blind, both will fall into a pit'" (Matthew 15:13–14).
- When you are unwelcomed, leave quietly. "But when you enter a town and are not welcomed, go into its streets and say, 'Even the dust of your town we wipe from our feet as a

warning to you. Yet be sure of this: The kingdom of God has come near'" (Luke 10:10–11).

- Let your peace (from Jesus) direct you to your support. "When you enter a house, first say, 'Peace to this house.' If someone who promotes peace is there, your peace will rest on them; if not, it will return to you. Stay there, eating and drinking whatever they give you, for the worker deserves his wages. Do not move around from house to house" (Luke 10:5–7).
- Expect changes in the Lord's methods. "Then Jesus asked them, 'When I sent you without purse, bag or sandals, did you lack anything?' 'Nothing,' they answered. He said to them, 'But now if you have a purse, take it, and also a bag; and if you don't have a sword, sell your cloak and buy one'" (Luke 22:35–36).

Lesson 31: Promise of Rewards for Faithful Workers

- There are great rewards for godly obedience when you are dealing with enemies. "But love your enemies, do good to them, and lend to them without expecting to get anything back. Then your reward will be great, and you will be children of the Most High, because he is kind to the ungrateful and wicked" (Luke 6:35).
- He who reaps draws wages. "Even now the one who reaps draws a wage and harvests a crop for eternal life, so that the sower and the reaper may be glad together" (John 4:36).
- A prophet's or righteous man's rewards can be received. "Whoever welcomes a prophet as a prophet will receive a prophet's reward, and whoever welcomes a righteous person as a righteous person will receive a righteous person's reward" (Matthew 10:41).
- What each person has done affects his rewards. "For the Son of Man is going to come in his Father's glory with his angels, and then he will reward each person according to what they have done" (Matthew 16:27).
- Even a cup of cold water is rewarded. "And if anyone gives even a cup of cold water to one of these little ones who is my

disciple, truly I tell you, that person will certainly not lose their reward" (Matthew 10:42).
- Faithful servants will share Christ's authority and joy. "His master replied, 'Well done, good and faithful servant! You have been faithful with a few things; I will put you in charge of many things. Come and share your master's happiness'" (Matthew 25:21).
- Good, trustworthy servants will receive more authority. "'Well done, my good servant!' his master replied. 'Because you have been trustworthy in a very small matter, take charge of ten cities'" (Luke 19:17).

Lesson 32: Command to Serve God and Man

- Settle matters with opponents quickly. "Settle matters quickly with your adversary who is taking you to court. Do it while you are still together on the way, or your adversary may hand you over to the judge, and the judge may hand you over to the officer, and you may be thrown into prison" (Matthew 5:25).
- Walk your talk. "But I tell you, do not swear an oath at all: either by heaven, for it is God's throne; or by the earth, for it is his footstool; or by Jerusalem, for it is the city of the Great King. And do not swear by your head, for you cannot make even one hair white or black. All you need to say is simply 'Yes' or 'No'; anything beyond this comes from the evil one" (Matthew 5:34–37).
- Keep your agreements. "And said, 'For this reason a man will leave his father and mother and be united to his wife, and the two will become one flesh.' So they are no longer two, but one flesh. Therefore what God has joined together, let no one separate" (Matthew 19:5–6).
- Do not stop others who minister in Jesus's name. "'Do not stop him,' Jesus said. 'For no one who does a miracle in my name can in the next moment say anything bad about me, for whoever is not against us is for us'" (Mark 9:39–40).

- Give to each what is due them. "Then Jesus said to them, 'Give back to Caesar what is Caesar's and to God what is God's.' And they were amazed at him" (Mark 12:17).
- Eat what is provided by your supporters. "When you enter a town and are welcomed, eat what is offered to you" (Luke 10:8).
- Waste nothing. "When they had all had enough to eat, he said to his disciples, 'Gather the pieces that are left over. Let nothing be wasted'" (John 6:12).

Lesson 33: Promise to One who Gives Generously

- Secret giving brings the Father's rewards. "But when you give to the needy, do not let your left hand know what your right hand is doing, so that your giving may be in secret. Then your Father, who sees what is done in secret, will reward you" (Matthew 6:3–4).
- One's giving measure becomes His receiving measure. "Give, and it will be given to you. A good measure, pressed down, shaken together and running over, will be poured into your lap. For with the measure you use, it will be measured to you" (Luke 6:38).
- Giving to the poor is a cleansing agent. "But now as for what is inside you—be generous to the poor, and everything will be clean for you" (Luke 11:41).
- Give to become eternally welcomed. "I tell you, use worldly wealth to gain friends for yourselves, so that when it is gone, you will be welcomed into eternal dwellings" (Luke 16:9).
- Giving brings more blessings than receiving does. "In everything I did, I showed you that by this kind of hard work we must help the weak, remembering the words the Lord Jesus himself said: 'It is more blessed to give than to receive'" (Acts 20:35).
- Giving to the poor brings God's resurrection blessings. "But when you give a banquet, invite the poor, the crippled, the lame, the blind, and you will be blessed. Although they cannot repay you, you will be repaid at the resurrection of the righteous" (Luke 14:13–14).

- Selling things to give to the poor brings heavenly treasure. "Jesus looked at him and loved him. 'One thing you lack,' he said. 'Go, sell everything you have and give to the poor, and you will have treasure in heaven. Then come, follow me'" (Mark 10:21).

Lesson 34: Command to Live and Speak Truth in Love

- Make peace with others "Therefore, if you are offering your gift at the altar and there remember that your brother or sister has something against you, leave your gift there in front of the altar. First go and be reconciled to them; then come and offer your gift" (Matthew 5:23–24).
- Do not look down on the immature. "See that you do not despise one of these little ones. For I tell you that their angels in heaven always see the face of my Father in heaven" (Matthew 18:10).
- Confront others in love and resolve offenses. "If your brother or sister sins, go and point out their fault, just between the two of you. If they listen to you, you have won them over. But if they will not listen, take one or two others along, so that 'every matter may be established by the testimony of two or three witnesses.' If they still refuse to listen, tell it to the church; and if they refuse to listen even to the church, treat them as you would a pagan or a tax collector" (Matthew 18:15–17).
- Forgive instead of condemning. "Do not judge and you will not be judged. Do not condemn, and you will not be condemned. Forgive, and you will be forgiven" (Luke 6:37).
- Forgive those who repent. "Jesus answered, 'I tell you, not seven times, but seventy-seven times'" (Matthew 18:22).
- Evaluate all things righteously. "Do not judge, or you too will be judged. For in the same way you judge others, you will be judged, and with the measure you use, it will be measured to you" (Matthew 7:1–2).
- Love each other as Jesus loved. "My command is this: Love each other as I have loved you" (John 15:12).

Lesson 35: Promise for Citizens of God's Kingdom

- They receive kingdom secrets. "He replied, 'Because the knowledge of the secrets of the kingdom of heaven has been given to you, but not to them'" (Matthew 13:11).
- Keys to the kingdom of heaven. "I will give you the keys of the kingdom of heaven; whatever you bind on earth will be bound in heaven, and whatever you loose on earth will be loosed in heaven" (Matthew 16:19).
- Know the signs of the coming King's nearness. "Even so, when you see these things happening, you know that the kingdom of God is near" (Luke 21:31).
- Our Father is pleased to give His kingdom to His family. "Do not be afraid, little flock, for your Father has been pleased to give you the kingdom" (Luke 12:32).
- The blessed of God inherit a prepared kingdom. "Then the King will say to those on his right, 'Come, you who are blessed by my Father; take your inheritance, the kingdom prepared for you since the creation of the world'" (Matthew 25:34).
- The righteous shine like the sun. "Then the righteous will shine like the sun in the kingdom of their Father. Whoever has ears, let them hear" (Matthew 13:43).
- Jesus will share the new covenant wine. "I tell you, I will not drink from this fruit of the vine from now on until that day when I drink it new with you in my Father's kingdom" (Matthew 26:29).

Lesson 36: Command to Walk What We Talk

- Secretly give to the needy. "Be careful not to practice your righteousness in front of others to be seen by them. If you do, you will have no reward from your Father in heaven. So when you give to the needy, do not announce it with trumpets, as the hypocrites do in the synagogues and on the streets, to be honored by others. Truly, I tell you, they have received their reward in full. But when you give to the

needy, do not let your left hand know what your right hand is doing" (Matthew 6:1–3).
- Pray secretly. "And when you pray, do not be like the hypocrites, for they love to pray standing in the synagogues and on the street corners to be seen by others. Truly, I tell you, they have received their reward in full. But when you pray, go into your room, close the door and pray to your Father, who is unseen. Then your Father, who sees what is done in secret, will reward you" (Matthew 6:5–6).
- Fast secretly. "When you fast, do not look somber as the hypocrites do, for they disfigure their faces to show others they are fasting. Truly, I tell you, they have received their reward in full. But when you fast, put oil on your head and wash your face, so that it will not be obvious to others that you are fasting, but only to your Father, who is unseen; and your Father, who sees what is done in secret, will reward you" (Matthew 6:16–18).
- Practice what you preach. "The teachers of the law and the Pharisees sit in Moses' seat. So you must be careful to do everything they tell you. But do not do what they do, for they do not practice what they preach" (Matthew 23:2–3).
- Guard yourself against all hypocrisy. "Meanwhile, when a crowd of many thousands had gathered, so that they were trampling on one another, Jesus began to speak first to his disciples, saying: 'Be on your guard against the yeast of the Pharisees, which is hypocrisy'" (Luke 12:1).
- Have no pride. Simply serve. "Beware of the teachers of the law. They like to walk around in flowing robes and love to be greeted with respect in the marketplaces and have the most important seats in the synagogues and the places of honor at banquets. They devour widows' houses and for a show make lengthy prayers. These men will be punished most severely" (Luke 20:46–47).
- Retain the heavenly Father's purpose in all things. "To those who sold doves he said, 'Get these out of here! Stop turning my Father's house into a market'" (John 2:16).

Lesson 37: Promise for Applying Belief

- Everything is possible for the believer. "'If you can?' said Jesus. 'Everything is possible for one who believes'" (Mark 9:23).
- Nothing will be impossible. "He replied, 'Because you have so little faith. Truly, I tell you, if you have faith as small as a mustard seed, you can say to this mountain, "Move from here to there," and it will move. Nothing will be impossible for you'" (Matthew 17:20).
- Faith the size of a mustard seed causes uprooting and planting. "He replied, 'If you have faith as small as a mustard seed, you can say to this mulberry tree, "Be uprooted and planted in the sea," and it will obey you'" (Luke 17:6).
- Faith in God with no doubting can move mountains. "'Have faith in God,' Jesus answered. 'Truly I tell you, if anyone says to this mountain, "Go, throw yourself into the sea," and does not doubt in their heart but believes that what they say will happen, it will be done for them'" (Mark 11:22–23).
- Complete faith includes belief of future receiving. "Therefore I tell you, whatever you ask for in prayer, believe that you have received it, and it will be yours" (Mark 11:24).
- To see the glory of God, one must believe. "Then Jesus said, 'Did I not tell you that if you believe, you will see the glory of God?'" (John 11:40).
- Greater things can be done by faith. "Very truly I tell you, whoever believes in me will do the works I have been doing, and they will do even greater things than these, because I am going to the Father" (John 14:12).

Lesson 38: Command to Fear Not but to Live in Faith

- Do not worry about life's essentials. "Therefore I tell you, do not worry about your life, what you will eat or drink; or about your body, what you will wear. Is not life more than food, and the body more than clothes?" (Matthew 6:25).

- Take courage. Recognize Jesus is with us. "But Jesus immediately said to them: 'Take courage! It is I. Don't be afraid'" (Matthew 14:27).
- Do not fear man or the Devil but do fear God. "I tell you, my friends, do not be afraid of those who kill the body and after that can do no more. But I will show you whom you should fear: Fear him who, after your body has been killed, has authority to throw you into hell. Yes, I tell you, fear him" (Luke 12:4–5).
- Faith in God can move mountains. "'Have faith in God,' Jesus answered. 'Truly I tell you, if anyone says to this mountain, "Go, throw yourself into the sea," and does not doubt in their heart but believes that what they say will happen, it will be done for them'" (Mark 11:22–23).
- Do not worry about food and drink. "And do not set your heart on what you will eat or drink; do not worry about it" (Luke 12:29).
- Do not let your hearts be troubled or afraid. "Peace I leave with you; my peace I give you. I do not give to you as the world gives. Do not let your hearts be troubled and do not be afraid" (John 14:27).
- Instead of doubting, believe in Jesus. "Then he said to Thomas, 'Put your finger here; see my hands. Reach out your hand and put it into my side. Stop doubting and believe'" (John 20:27).

Lesson 39: Promise to Those in Close Relationship with Jesus Christ

- Jesus seeks a close relationship. "Here I am! I stand at the door and knock. If anyone hears my voice and opens the door, I will come in and eat with that person, and they with me" (Revelation 3:20).
- Jesus desires to provide abundant life. "I am the gate; whoever enters through me will be saved. They will come in and go out, and find pasture. The thief comes only to steal and kill and destroy; I have come that they may have life, and have it to the full" (John 10:9–10).

- One in God's will can discern Christ's teachings. "Anyone who chooses to do the will of God will find out whether my teaching comes from God or whether I speak on my own" (John 7:17).
- Jesus's yoke relationship produces soul rest. "Come to me, all you who are weary and burdened, and I will give you rest. Take my yoke upon you and learn from me, for I am gentle and humble in heart, and you will find rest for your souls. For my yoke is easy and my burden is light" (Matthew 11:28–30).
- Jesus's own peace can be enjoyed by His family. "Peace I leave with you; my peace I give you. I do not give to you as the world gives. Do not let your hearts be troubled and do not be afraid" (John 14:27).
- Complete joy of the Lord comes from obeying Jesus. "If you keep my commands, you will remain in my love, just as I have kept my Father's commands and remain in his love. I have told you this so that my joy may be in you and that your joy may be complete" (John 15:10–11).
- The gates of Hades will not conquer Jesus's church. "And I tell you that you are Peter, and on this rock I will build my church, and the gates of Hades will not overcome it" (Matthew 16:18).

Lesson 40: Command to Be Christlike in My Own Circle

- To enter life, obey His commandments. "'Why do you ask me about what is good?' Jesus replied. 'There is only One who is good. If you want to enter life, keep the commandments'" (Matthew 19:17).
- Do not murder. "Jesus replied, 'You shall not murder'" (Matthew 19:18).
- Do not commit adultery "Jesus replied, you shall not commit adultery" (Matthew 19:18).
- Do not steal. "Jesus replied, you shall not steal" (Matthew 19:18).
- Do not lie. "Jesus replied, you shall not give false testimony" (Matthew 19:18).

- Honor your father and mother. "Honor your father and mother, and love your neighbor as yourself" (Matthew 19:19)
- Do good to others. "Do to others as you would have them do to you" (Luke 6:31).

Lesson 41: Promise to One Who Overcomes Temptations to Sin

- Overcomers will eat of paradise's Tree of Life. "Whoever has ears let them hear what the Spirit says to the churches. To the one who is victorious, I will give the right to eat from the tree of life, which is in the paradise of God" (Revelation 2:7).
- Overcomers will not be hurt by the second death. "He that hath an ear, let him hear what the Spirit says to the churches; He that overcomes shall not be hurt of the second death" (Revelation 2:11).
- Overcomers receive hidden manna and name stones. "Whoever has ears, let them hear what the Spirit says to the churches. To the one who is victorious, I will give some of the hidden manna. I will also give that person a white stone with a new name written on it, known only to the one who receives it" (Revelation 2:17).
- Overcomers receive authority over nations. "To the one who is victorious and does my will to the end, I will give authority over the nations—that one 'will rule them with an iron scepter and will dash them to pieces like pottery'—just as I have received authority from my Father. I will also give that one the morning star" (Revelation 2:26–28).
- Overcomers will be acknowledged before the Father and angels. "The one who is victorious will, like them, be dressed in white. I will never blot out the name of that person from the book of life, but will acknowledge that name before my Father and his angels" (Revelation 3:5).
- Overcomers will become posts in God's temple. "The one who is victorious I will make a pillar in the temple of my God. Never again will they leave it. I will write on them the name of my God and the name of the city of my God, the

new Jerusalem, which is coming down out of heaven from my God; and I will also write on them my new name" (Revelation 3:12).
- Overcomers will sit with Jesus on His throne. "To the one who is victorious, I will give the right to sit with me on my throne, just as I was victorious and sat down with my Father on his throne" (Revelation 3:21).

Lesson 42: Command to Finish the Course

- When insulted, persecuted, and lied about because of Jesus, rejoice. "Blessed are you when people insult you, persecute you and falsely say all kinds of evil against you because of me. Rejoice and be glad, because great is your reward in heaven, for in the same way they persecuted the prophets who were before you" (Matthew 5:11–12). "Rejoice in that day and leap for joy, because great is your reward in heaven. For that is how their ancestors treated the prophets" (Luke 6:23).
- Do not worry about what to say. "But when they arrest you, do not worry about what to say or how to say it. At that time, you will be given what to say" (Matthew 10:19).
- Traveling ministers are to leave when persecuted. "When you are persecuted in one place, flee to another. Truly, I tell you, you will not finish going through the towns of Israel before the Son of Man comes" (Matthew 10:23).
- When severity comes, expectantly look for my Redeemer. "When these things begin to take place, stand up and lift up your heads, because your redemption is drawing near" (Luke 21:28).
- Stop grumbling. "'Stop grumbling among yourselves,' Jesus answered" (John 6:43).
- Do not fear suffering or persecution. Receive your crown. "Do not be afraid of what you are about to suffer. I tell you, the devil will put some of you in prison to test you, and you will suffer persecution for ten days. Be faithful, even to the point of death, and I will give you life as your victor's crown" (Revelation 2:10).

- Hold on to your faith. Protect your crown. "I am coming soon. Hold on to what you have, so that no one will take your crown" (Revelation 3:11).

Chapter 12– New Covenant Term Five

I Spiritually Wash Regularly to Remain Useful to God

The study of sin is central to Christianity, since its basic message is about redemption from sin provided by Jesus Christ. In your personal search to become Christlike on the earth, you must identify and remove yourself from everything that is unlike Christ. Sin is everything that is not Christlike.

Jesus Christ is Holy and never sinned. The following list can help you to become Christlike by seeking to stop every un-Christlike thought or behavior. This list records what Jesus and the apostles defined as sins in the New Testament portion of the KJV Bible.

The significance of sin is demonstrated by Jesus Christ's sacrificial death, to completely pay for each of our sins. Since the Lord Jesus Christ teaches that sin in one's life breaks close fellowship with God, a list of sins is very important. Because the New Covenant of Jesus Christ provides for my complete cleansing from every sin, I try to quickly wash away my guilt as soon as I am aware of them (Matthew 15:18–23; Galatians 6:1–2). Then my friend who hears me confess my sins to the heavenly Father can assure me of forgiveness and cleansing (James 5:16–20).

"If we confess our sins, he is faithful and just and will forgive us our sins and purify us from all unrighteousness"(1 John 1:9).

"Those who cleanse themselves…will be instruments for special purposes, made holy, useful to the Master and prepared to do any good work" (2 Timothy 2:21).

Jesus Christ's blood sacrifice was accepted by almighty God as the full payment for the sins of each person who enters into God's New Covenant. Jesus said this about His own blood sacrifice, "This is my blood of the New Covenant, which is poured out for many for the forgiveness of sins" (Matthew 26:28).

God's way for each New Covenant member to overcome every temptation and stop each sin is described in Chapter 14, *God's Five-Step Power Sin Wash.*

How to Use the Sin List

Since the Lord Jesus Christ teaches that sin in one's life breaks close fellowship with God, a list of sins becomes very important. This section records every sin found in the New Testament portion of the King James Translation of the Holy Bible.

Because the New Covenant of Jesus Christ provides for my complete cleansing from every sin, I try to quickly wash away my guilt, as soon as I am aware of it. (Matthew 15:18–23, Galatians 6:1–2). Then my friend who hears me confess to the heavenly Father my sins, can assure me of my forgiveness and cleansing by reminding me that, "If we confess our sins, he is faithful and just and will forgive us our sins and purify us from all unrighteousness" (1 John 1:9).

More information is available in Chapter 16, "Gentle Restoration: God's Way to Wash Away Sin-Guilt".

(Many thanks to Patricia Hulsey of Harvestime.org for use of this sin list and many other free resources for spreading the Kingdom of God. *Harvestime* materials have been well received by our friends since 2010.)

The Sin List

Each KJV word for a sin in the New Testament is followed by brief definitions, and references.

- Abominable idolatry—worship, adore, revere anything except God is detestable, offensive, terrible (1 Peter 4:2).

- Abominable—the vile, repulsive, horrible (Revelation 21:8).

- Adultery—sexual infidelity or disloyalty (1 Timothy 1:9; Matthew 15:18; Mark 7:21; 1 Corinthians 6:9; Galatians 5:19).

- Alienated from godliness through ignorance—separated from godly living without knowing it (Ephesians 4:17).

- Anger—fury, rage (Ephesians 4:25; Colossians 3:5).

- Any kind of impurity—contamination, pollution (Ephesians 5:3).

- Approval of those who sin (Romans 1:29).

- Arrogance—conceit, haughtiness, pride (Mark 7:21; Roman 1:29).

- Backbiting—slander, insult, smear (2 Corinthians 12:20).

- Banqueting—carousing, wild parties (1 Peter 4:2).

- Bitterness—resentment, sullenness, sourness (Ephesians 4:25).

- Blasphemer—abusive, to swear, to curse (2 Timothy 3:1).

- Blindness of the heart—loss of insight, insensitive (Ephesians 4:17).

- Boastful—arrogant, bragging (Romans 1:29; 2 Timothy 3:1).

- Busybody in other's matters—meddler, gossip, bigmouth (1 Peter 4:21).

- Clamor—shout, scream, bawl (Ephesians 4:25).

- Coarse—vulgar, crude, rude, bad mannered (Ephesians 5:3).

- Continue these sins (Roman 1:29).

- Corrupt—dishonest, crooked, unwholesome (Ephesians 4:25).

- Covetous–envious, jealous, greedy for money (Ephesians 5:5; 2 Timothy 3:1).

- Darkened understanding—dim awareness, poor insight (Ephesians 4:17, 22).

- Debates–quarreling, argue, dispute (2 Corinthians 12:20; 2 Timothy 2:23–24).

- Debauchery–wickedness, depravity, corruption (Romans 13:13).

- Deceit—dishonesty, trickery, pretense (Mark 7:21; Romans 1:29).

- Deceived—mislead, tricked, swindled (Titus 3:3).

- Depravity—immorality, wickedness (Romans 1:29).

- Despisers of those who are good—looking down on or hating people who do good (2 Timothy 3:1).

- Disobedient—rebel at or defy authorities (Romans 1:29; 2 Timothy 3:1; Titus 3:3).

- Dissension–rebellion, opposition (Romans 13:13).

- Dogs—homosexuals (Philippians 3:2; Revelation 22:14).

- Drunkard—intoxicated, high, inebriated (Romans 13:13; 1 Corinthians 5:9; 1 Corinthians 6:9; Galatians 5:19).

- Emulations—copying bad, corrupt lifestyles (Galatians 5:19).

- Envy (Mark 7:21; Romans 1:29; 2 Corinthians 12:20; Galatians 5:19; 1 Peter 2:1).

- Every kind of wickedness (Romans 1:29).

- Evil desires (Colossians 3:5).

- Evil jealousy—resentment (Romans 1:29).

- Evil speaking—wicked, slanderous, sinful words (Ephesians 4:25; 1 Peter 2:1).

- Evil thoughts—wicked beliefs, opinions, or viewpoints (Matthew 15:18; Mark 7:21).

- Evildoer—one being wicked or in crime (1 Peter 4:2).

- Excess of wine—overindulgence, drunkenness (1 Peter 4:2).

- Faithless—disloyal, fickle, unfaithful (Romans 1:29).

- False accusers—counterfeit blamers, fake, phony charges (2 Timothy 3:1).

- False testimony—faked, made up evidence (Matthew 15:18).

- Fearful—frightened, anxious, timid, cowardly (Revelation 21:8).

- Fierce—violent, brutal, vicious (2 Timothy 3:1).

- Filthy language—dirty, smutty words (Colossians 3:5).

- Folly—foolishness, craziness (Mark 7:21–22).

- Foolish talk—silly, unwise words (Ephesians 5:3–4; Titus 3:3).

- Form of godliness but denying its power—not showing God's way to become holy (2 Timothy 3:5).

- Fornication—sexual immorality (Galatians 5:19).

- Giving place to the Devil—letting any evil continue (Ephesians 4:25–27).

- God haters—those who detest or cannot stand the Creator (Romans 1:29).

- Gossips—telling rumors, hearsay, chitchat (Romans 1:29–30).

- Gratify sinful, natural desires—thoughtlessly satisfying one's selfish wants (Romans 13:13–14).

- Greed—excessive, self-indulgence (Ephesians 5:3–5; Colossians 3:5).

- Grieving the Holy Spirit—causing sorrow or mourning for the Holy Spirit (Ephesians 4:30).

- Guile—cunning, slyness, craftiness, deceit (1 Peter 2:1).

- Harm to my body—physical damage, hurt, injury (1 Corinthians 3:16–17, 6:19–20).

- Hatred—disgust, extreme dislike (Galatians 5:19–20; Titus 3:3).

- Heady—thrilling, exciting, exhilarating (2 Timothy 3:4).

- Heartless—callous, cruel, unfeeling, unkind (Romans 1:29–31).

- Heresies—false teaching, deviation from the Bible's truth (Galatians 5:19; 2 Peter 2:1).

- High-minded—conceited, self-important, vain, stuck-up (2 Timothy 3:1–3).

- Hint of sexual immorality—any slight implication or appearance of wickedness (Ephesians 5:3).

- Homosexuals—abnormal, not normal sexual relations (1 Corinthians 6:9).

- Hypocrisy—double standards, two-facedness, and insincerity (1 Peter 2:1).

- Idolatry—worship, adoration, and reverence for anything other than God (1 Corinthians 6:9; Galatians 5:19–20; Ephesians 5:5; Colossians 3:5; Revelation 21:8, 22:14).

- Immoral—wicked, depraved, corrupt, dishonest (1 Corinthians 5:9–10).

- Impurity—contamination, pollution, uncleanness, dirtiness (Colossians 3:5).

- Incontinent—without self-control (2 Timothy 3:1–3).

- Insolent—rude, disrespectful (Romans 1:29).

- Invent ways to do evil—create, originate, devise any different sinful behavior (Romans 1:29).

- Irreligious—ungodly, profane, blasphemous, unspiritual (1 Timothy 1:9).

- Jealousy— protectiveness, envy, covetousness, resentment (Romans 13:13).

- Killers of parents—murderer, slayer of close relative (1 Timothy 1:9).

- Lasciviousness—wickedness, decadence, corruption (Galatians 5:19; Ephesians 4:17; 1 Peter 4:2–4).

- Lawbreakers—criminal, crook, felon, convict (1 Timothy 1:9).

- Lewdness—filthiness, coarseness, vulgarity, profanity, uncouthness (Mark 7:21–22).

- Liars—fraud, fake, pretender, impostor, phony (1 Timothy 1:9; Revelation 21:8).

- Living in envy—jealous, greedy, resentful lifestyle (Titus 3:3).

- Living in malice—hateful, mean, nasty, wicked, cruel lifestyle (Titus 3:3).

- Lovers of pleasures rather than God (2 Timothy 3:4).

- Lovers of themselves—a fan, follower, devotee, supporter of one's self (2 Timothy 3:1–4).

- Lust—to yearn, desire, long, or ache for (Colossians 3:5; 1 Peter 4:2–3).

- Lying—untruthful, dishonest, deceitful (Ephesians 4:25, 3:5).

- Male prostitutes—a man paid for sexual relations (1 Corinthians 6:9).

- Malice—hatred, spite, meanness, cruelty (Mark 7:21; Romans 1:29; Ephesians 4:25; Colossians 3:5; 1 Peter 2:1).

- Murder—kill, slay, put to death (Matthew 15:18; Mark 7:21; Romans 1:29; Galatians 5:19; 1 Timothy 1:9; 1 Peter 4:2; Revelation 21:8, 22:14).

- Obscenity—vulgarity, wickedness, crudity, indecency (Ephesians 5:3).

- Orgies—immoral, wicked, crude, drunken, unrestrained wild parties (Romans 13:13).

- Past feelings—insensitive, not felt, hardened, harsh (Ephesians 4:19).

- Perjurers lying when under oath, false swearing before a judge (1 Timothy 1:9).

- Perverts—sexually degenerate; they defile others in many terrible ways (1 Timothy 1:9).

- Proud—arrogant, self-righteous, overconfident (2 Timothy 3:1).

- Rage—rant and rave, frenzy, furious anger (Colossians3:5).

- Rebels—mutineer, radical, insurgent, disobedient (1 Timothy 1:9).

- Reveling—get drunk, wild party (Galatians 5:19; 1 Peter 4:2).

- Ruthless—cruel, callous, brutal, cold-blooded (Romans 1:29).

- Seditions—treason, causing a rebellion, troublemaking (Galatians 5:19).

- Senseless—pointless, ridiculous (Romans 1:29).

- Serving lusts and pleasures—enslaved by passions, delights, and happiness (Titus 3:3).

- Sexual immorality—sexual wickedness, corruption, depravity (Matthew 15:18, 7:21; Romans 13:13; 1 Corinthians 6:9; Colossians 3:5).

- Sinners—those who offend God and break God's laws, unholy, profane (1 Timothy 1:9).

- Slander—insult, slur, libel (Matthew 15:18; Mark 7:21; Romans 1:29; 1 Corinthians 5:9, 6:9; Colossians3:5).

- Slave traders—selling kidnapped people (1 Timothy 1:9).

- Sorcerers—wizards, witches practicing magic arts (Revelation 22:8, 14).

- Stealing—theft, robbery, burglary (Ephesians 4:25).

- Strife—conflict, discord, fighting, rivalry (Romans 1:29; 2 Corinthians 12:20; Galatians 5:19).

- Swellings—arrogance, puff up (2 Corinthians 12:20).

- Swindlers—cheat, trickster, crook, fraud (1 Corinthians 5:9, 6:9).

- Theft—robbery, stealing, shoplifting (Matthew 15:18; Mark 7:21; 1 Corinthians 6:9; 1 Peter 4:2).

- Traitors—turncoat, defector, deserter, treacherous (2 Timothy 3:1).

- Truce breakers—start wars, ruin the peace, cause fights (2 Timothy 3:1).

- Tumults—uproar, turmoil, confusion, chaos (2 Corinthians 12:20).

- Unbelieving—uncertain, doubting, suspicious (Revelation 21:8).

- Unclean—impure, dirty, infected (Galatians 5:19; Ephesians 4:17, 5:5).

- Ungodly—irreverent, sinful, wicked (1 Timothy 1:9; 2 Timothy 3:1).

- Unthankful—ungrateful, unappreciative (2 Timothy 3:1).

- Vain—ineffective, useless, worthless (Ephesians 4:17).

- Variance—inconsistency, conflict, clash (Galatians 5:19).

- Whispering—murmur, rumor, gossip (2 Corinthians 12:20).

- Whoremonger—immoral sexual activity (Ephesians 5:5; Revelation 21:8, 22:14).

- Whosoever loves to lie— all who love and practice falsehood (Revelation 22:15).

- Witchcraft—evil supernatural power worker (Galatians 5:19).

- Without natural affection—lacking, without normal love (2 Timothy 3:1).

- Wrath—anger, rage, fury (2 Corinthians 12:20; Galatians 5:19; Ephesians 4:25).

To help you avoid sin temptation and overcome every sin in your life, please read and apply Part 4, *Chapter 14, God's Five-Step Power Sin Wash.*

Part Four: Some Victory Principles of the Kingdom of God

Part Four is a collection of spiritual tools proven to resolve difficult or dramatic problems. Considering my introduction of these principles from the kingdom of God to others needing assistance, I am deeply touched as memories flood my heart of all the precious people of God restored to places of peace with their Creator by putting these tools into practice.

I encourage you to faithfully consider each item. These are practical steps used to bring a kingdom of God solution to normal recurring dilemmas in the lives of God's people. We realize that from the time of the fall from human sinful choice until now, five elements of human existence remain the same.

1. We have the same almighty God creator.

2. We have the same devil, Satan, in the Earth.

3. Earthly humans keep becoming more like their spiritual father, Satan.

4. Each generation of God's family struggles against the enlarging evil world power at that point in time.

5. Heavenly Father continuously reveals victorious principles and tools to His people.

Grateful persons who received almighty God's blessing frequently offer comments like this, "I've often read these familiar scriptures but have never seen them applied this way. The peaceful results are wonderful. Thank you for this powerful, precious insight that brought glory to God and clear spiritual victory over the frustrations we faced."

Chapter 13: Soul Rest to Hear the Holy Spirit

One of the most powerful Victory Principles is Soul Rest. Soul Rest is a rich treasure that Jesus Christ makes possible for you as He did for Jeremiah and King David (Jeremiah 6:16; Psalm 131:1–4). When you obey Jesus's commands you will begin to stay in daily Soul Rest receiving God's truths all day long.

Jesus explained that "God is spirit, and his worshipers must worship in spirit and in truth" (John 4:24). Today, almighty God wants to have this internal spiritual fellowship with each person. The Apostle Paul mentioned this spiritual fellowship in Romans 8:16, "The spirit himself testifies with our spirit that we are God's children."

Also, Lord Jesus Christ used the expression, "He who has an ear, let him hear what the Spirit says to the churches" (Revelation 2:7,11,17,29, 3:6,13,22).

You can learn to hear what Holy Spirit wants to tell you through your own spirit. In the New Covenant the Lord God offers, "I will give you a new heart and put a new spirit in you; I will remove from you your heart of stone and give you a heart if flesh. And will put my Spirit in you and move you to follow my decrees and be careful to keep my laws" (Ezekiel 36:26–27).

Soul Rest is a Tremendous Blessing

Satan deceived the first family (Adam and Eve) into breaking the terms of their covenant with God. One tragic consequence of their rebellion toward God was the separation from fellowship with Him. Adam and Eve could not hear God as well as they could before. Soul rest is one major tool to help resolve this problem. As you will learn, the Holy Spirit from God is actively working upon all humans on the earth (John 15:26, 16:8–11; Acts 2:17).

Christ's last words in Revelation seven times stress the expression "an ear to hear what the Spirit is saying." Quieting soul (mind, will, and emotion) assists me in developing an ear to hear the Holy Spirit.

A wonderful breakthrough and measurable increase in my consistent communication with Holy Spirit came from discovering and applying what the prophets and the Lord Jesus Christ and his apostles taught about rest for one's soul. It is very wise to deliberately start each day with a soul rest routine.

The prophet offers to teach the age-old daily steps (ancient path) of staying in soul rest, "ask for the ancient paths, ask where the good way is, and walk in it, and you will find rest for your souls" (Jeremiah 6:16).

Jesus Christ offered soul rest to those in relational discipleship with him, "you will find rest for your souls" (Matthew 11:29).

The apostle Paul mentions a consistent fellowship with Holy Spirit, "the fellowship of the Holy Spirit be with you all" (2 Corinthians 13:14 NLT) and, "fellowship together in the Spirit" (Philippians 2:1 NLT).

"The Spirit himself testifies with our spirit that we are God's children" (Romans 8:16).

What Is Soul Rest?

Soul rest, as defined in this book, is a way of living in peace in the midst of one's daily life, whether it is active and hectic, catastrophic or boring, exciting or dull. A part of soul rest includes developing the fruit of the Spirit (Galatians 5). As with all trees, good fruit comes with the help of the laborer. Jesus commanded His followers to make their trees good or bad. Spiritual fruit is developed through the habitual choices of each Christian. Peace and self-control are fruits that relate to the development of soul rest.

God's Word shows that it is the responsibility of each child of God to calm down our own demanding minds, wills, and emotions and to stop the unnecessary demands of our bodies. This can be done through the power of the Holy Spirit, who lives in the believer. By the practice of walking in soul rest, our human spirit can hear the still, small voice of the Holy Spirit more routinely. The Holy Spirit lives within the heart of God's child and wants to reveal the things of God regularly (2 Corinthians 1:21–22; Galatians 4:6).

To state this personally, the Spirit of truth, the Counselor living forever within me, a child of God, wants to teach me all that I need, remind me of what I need, and reveal to me things that are to come (John 14:16–17, 26,16:13).

The Holy Spirit is trying to speak Jesus's message regularly to my own human spirit, but I must develop my spiritual ears to hear what the Holy Spirit is saying (Romans 8:16; 1 Corinthians 2:9–12; Revelation 2:7, 11, 17, 29, 3:6, 13, 22).

Chapter 14: God's Five-Step Power Sin Wash

The Bible teaches that all sin temptations can be avoided, and all sin-enslavements can be victoriously overcome as a member of the New Covenant of God. Practice *God's Five-Step Power Sin Wash* whenever a sinful stronghold or addiction continuously enslaves a member of God's New Covenant. Be encouraged to carefully learn and practice these steps. Enjoy the freedom and peace that the New Covenant from God offers.

Introduction

These five specific steps presented in this chapter, taken from 2 Timothy 2:19–26, enable a member of the New Covenant to:

- *Cleanse* themselves from sin,
- *Flee* (overcome) sin-temptations,
- *Pursue* right things with a pure hearted friend while avoiding arguments and quarrels,
- *Receive* a Godly *repentant* heart that accepts knowledge of truth to regain their senses,
- *Escape* (set themselves free) from the devil's sin-captivity.

Key Scripture

"In a large house there are articles not only of gold and silver, but also of wood and clay; some are for special purposes and some for common use. Those who *cleanse* themselves from the latter will be instruments for special purposes, made holy, useful to the Master and prepared to do any good work. *Flee* the evil desires of youth and pursue righteousness, faith, love and peace, along with those who call on the Lord out of a pure heart. Don't have anything to do with foolish and stupid arguments, because you know they produce quarrels. And the Lord's servant must not be quarrelsome but must be kind to everyone, able to teach, not resentful. Opponents must be gently instructed, in the hope that God will grant them repentance leading them to a knowledge of the truth, and that they will come to their senses and *escape* from the trap of the devil, who has taken them captive to do his will" (2 Timothy 2:20–26).

Real Life Application of These Five Steps

To Cleanse. *I cleanse myself each time I am convicted of a sin.* I confess and express to almighty God my decision to stop each sin completely and receive God's forgiveness, confirmed by a witness (Matthew 18:15–18; John 20:22–23; 1 Corinthians 6:9–11; Galatians 6:1–2; James 5:16; 1 John 1:9;Revelation 22:14)

To Flee. *To avoid each temptation outwardly,* I contact my pure hearted friend to assist me evade that sin, not give into the temptation and put my mind on something good and right. Inwardly, by the stronger power of Holy Spirit, I resist the devil's short temptation-suffering and receive God's strong, firm and unwavering restoration (I John 4:4; 1 Peter 5:8–11).

From repeating these steps every time I need them, the Holy Spirit completely puts to death each of my sin strongholds and misdeeds (Romans 8:13).

To Pursue Righteous Truth. My pure hearted friend helps me discover God's truth to replace the devil's sin-deception and to stay on God's narrow road to eternal life (Matthew 7:14; James 5:19–20). This servant-friend never quarrels, argues or resents spiritually washing my feet repeatedly. He gently instructs me with patience, knowing full well that only God can change my heart.

Repentance. *When God gives me a repentant heart to understand His truth,* I recover my good sense and see how dumb the devil's deceptive lie really is. (2 Corinthians 3:2–3; Ezekiel 36:26–27).

Escape. Then I escape from the devil's lie-trap by my firm decision to believe and stand on God's truth. By continuing to repeat God's Five-Step Power Sin Wash, I actually do "escape from the trap of the devil" (2 Timothy 2:19–26).

All Temptation Can Be Avoided (What a great way to live.)

"No temptation has overtaken you except what is common to mankind. And God is faithful; he will not let you be tempted beyond what you can bear. But when you are tempted, he will also provide a way out so that you can endure it" (1 Corinthians 10:13).

"And lead us not into temptation, but deliver us from the evil one" (Matthew 6:13).

"Watch and pray so that you will not fall into temptation" (Matthew 26:41).

All Sin Can Be Overcome (Being set free and remaining free. Yippee!)

"May God himself, the God of peace, sanctify you through and through? May your whole spirit, soul and body be kept blameless at the coming of our Lord Jesus Christ? The one who calls you is faithful, and he will do it" (1 Thessalonians 5:23–24).

Four Common Categories of Sin

"Now these things occurred as examples to keep us from setting our hearts on evil things as they did.

[1] Do not be idolaters, as some of them were; as it is written: "The people sat down to eat and drink and got up to indulge in revelry."

2] We should not commit sexual immorality, as some of them did—and in one day twenty-three thousand of them died.

[3] We should not test Christ, as some of them did—and were killed by snakes.

[4] And do not grumble, as some of them did—and were killed by the destroying angel.

These things happened to them as examples and were written down as warnings for us, on whom the culmination of the ages has come. So, if you think you are standing firm, be careful that you don't fall. No temptation has overtaken you except what is common to mankind. And God is faithful; he will not let you be tempted beyond what you can bear. But when you are tempted, he will also provide a way out so that you can endure it" (1Corinthians 10:6–13).

Examining Ourselves and Stopping Our Sin Prevents Much Sickness and Early Death

"Everyone ought to examine themselves before they eat of the bread and drink from the cup. For those who eat and drink without discerning the body of Christ eat and drink judgment on themselves. That is why many among you are weak and sick, and a number of you have fallen asleep. But if we were more discerning with regard to ourselves, we would not come under such judgment. Nevertheless, when we are judged in this way by the Lord, we are being disciplined so that we will not be finally condemned with the world" (1 Corinthians 11:28–32).

Chapter 15: My Special Tool Design Made in His Image

We are created and designed to be worker-tools or vessels for God's use (1 Corinthians 3:9–15; Ephesians 2:10; Timothy 2:14, 21). Let us look at God's original created design of us as His tool, the Devil's damaging effects upon us, and God's tool redesign through Lord Jesus Christ.

Original Tool Design

It is significant for us to understand what God had in mind when He created humanity. In the beginning, having been made in God's image, man and woman carried out successful teamwork and enjoyed a shame-free relationship with each other and God (Genesis 1:26–31, 2:4–10, 15–25). They were servants (tools) of righteousness, obediently doing the work God designed them to do.

"Then God said, "Let us make mankind in our image, in our likeness, so that they may rule over the fish in the sea and the birds in the sky, over the livestock and all the wild animals, and over all the creatures that move along the ground." So God created mankind in his own image, in the image of God he created them; male and female he created them. God blessed them and said to them, "Be fruitful and increase in number; fill the earth and subdue it. Rule over the fish in the sea and the birds in the sky and over every living creature that moves on the ground." Then God said, "I give you every seed-bearing plant on the face of the whole earth and every tree that has fruit with seed in it. They will be yours for food. And to all the beasts of the earth and all the birds in the sky and all the creatures that move along the ground—everything that has the breath of life in it—I give every green plant for food." And it was so" (Genesis 1:26–40).

"Then the LORD God formed a man from the dust of the ground and breathed into his nostrils the breath of life, and the man became a living being. Now the LORD God had planted a garden in the east, in Eden; and there he put the man he had formed. The LORD

God made all kinds of trees grow out of the ground—trees that were pleasing to the eye and good for food. The LORD God took the man and put him in the Garden of Eden to work it and take care of it. The LORD God said, "It is not good for the man to be alone. I will make a helper suitable for him." Now the LORD God had formed out of the ground all the wild animals and all the birds in the sky. He brought them to the man to see what he would name them; and whatever the man called each living creature, that was its name. So the man gave names to all the livestock, the birds in the sky and all the wild animals" (Genesis 2:1–25).

The Devil's Damaging Results

One consequence of the wrong tool usage is "tool-pusher disfiguration." When humanity chose to obey Satan, he enslaved them by his new spiritual authority as spiritual prince of the world. Humanity's spiritual heart and image became disfigured into evil from childhood (2 Corinthians 4:4; Ephesians 2:1–3; Genesis 6:5, 8:21; Psalm 51:5; Romans 1:21). Jesus explained how persons reflect their spiritual Father (John 8:38–47, 5:19).

This spiritual disobedience changed humanity. "God was sorry that he had made the human race in the first place; it broke his heart. God said, 'I'll get rid of my ruined creation, make a clean sweep. I'm sorry I made them'" (Genesis 6:6–7 MSG).

Here is a major question: Who do I actually work for? Satan or the Lord Jesus Christ? Let's remember that Jesus said Peter was being used by Satan (Matthew 4:10, 12:30; Mark 9:40; Luke 4:8,11:23; Romans 6:13, 16, 19, 12:1; 1 Corinthians 6:20).

Tool Redesign into Christ's Likeness

The Lord Jesus Christ defeated Satan. Because of God's great love and mercy, He paid the legal sin debt for humanity by Jesus's suffering, death, and resurrection. God judged as guilty the spiritual prince of the earth (John 3:8, 12:31, 14:30, 16:11; Hebrews 2:14–15). "All authority in heaven and on earth has been given to me" (Matthew 28:18).

From God's word we can gain amazing insights about the victorious future for those of us who keep the terms of almighty God's covenants. I particularly enjoy the following information about the New Earth and New Heaven government.

"Or do you not know that the Lord's people will judge the world? And if you are to judge the world, are you not competent to judge trivial cases? Do you not know that we will judge angels? How much more the things of this life!" (1 Corinthians 6:2–3).

"It is not to angels that he has subjected the world to come, about which we are speaking. But there is a place where someone has testified: "What is mankind that you are mindful of them, a son of man that you care for him? You made them a little lower than the angels; you crowned them with glory and honor and put everything under their feet." In putting everything under them, God left nothing that is not subject to them. Yet at present we do not see everything subject to them. But we do see Jesus, who was made lower than the angels for a little while, now crowned with glory and honor because he suffered death, so that by the grace of God he might taste death for everyone (Hebrews 2:5–9).

Jesus Christ Brought God's Long-Expected New Covenant to Earth

He saved us by His grace and changed each one in His family into babes in Christ; new creatures. A lifelong process begins at one's spiritual rebirth in which we can "put on the new man created in righteousness and true holiness." Each one of God's family should be in deliberate processes to "be conformed to the likeness of his Son" (Roman 8:29). "We can bring each person to maturity. To be mature is to be basic. Christ! No more, no less" (Colossians 1:28 MSG).

What Is the Spiritual Likeness of Christ?

Jesus humanly looked like an Israelite but spiritually looked like our heavenly Father. Therefore, as a member of God's spiritual family through Jesus Christ, my special tool redesign is to be spiritually like Jesus Christ (Hebrews 1:3; Colossians 1:15; 2 Corinthians 4:4; John 12:45, 14:9).

My Visible Body, My Invisible Soul, My Invisible Spirit, and My Invisible Heart

Now we turn to specifics concerning tool redesign and offer steps to receive the knowledge of God about humans as His workers. We must know how people really function in order to become effective agents of change for our Lord Jesus. Jesus told us how to observe people's spiritual image, and our brothers describe more details (John 7:24; 1 Samuel 16:7; Luke 16:15).

All reputable Bible scholars teach Christians to learn self-control as well as the other fruits of the Holy Spirit. Learning to appreciate and receive the continuous ministry of the Holy Spirit is difficult. Maximizing my tool redesign for the born-again child of God into Christ's likeness can become a daily reality when the choices of God's child are correct. To assist in all choices, God's child must have the Holy Spirit living in his or her heart and closely available as a daily guide, teacher, and empowering source on a 24/7 for 365 days per year (2 Corinthians 1:22, 5:5; Romans 8:23; Ephesians 1:13–14; Galatians 4:6).

Why Attempt to Define the Following Biblical Terms?

As an effective worker for God, you must have hands-on definitions and understanding of serious biblical terms in order to use God's truth. Here are some very short and simple definitions. Every human function is automatically operating together, but the following points, drawn from the Bible, are very valuable:

My invisible soul is eternal. It operates with my spirit and it is often called my personality.

- My mind is my thinker, my reasoning processes (how I think).
- My will is my chooser, my decision-making processes (how I choose).
- My emotions release my feelings (e.g., happiness, sadness, madness, sorrow, joy, etc.).

My invisible spirit is eternal. It operates with my soul, and it is my communicator with spirits when I am receiving spiritual gifts from the Holy Spirit or hearing evil voices, etc.

- My conscience automatically tells me right or wrong (mostly when awake).
- My intuition is my gut level knower without many facts (mostly when awake).
- My dreams are my spiritual receivers when my soul and body are at rest.
- My visions are my spiritual receivers when my soul and body are at rest.
- My invisible spirit is my communicator with God, angels/demons, or human's spirits—who put thoughts into my mind. I receive a new spirit from God's new covenant (Ezekiel 36:25–27; John 3:5–8; 1 John 1:9–10).

My invisible heart is eternal. It is the deepest inner spiritual portion of each human.

- It contains each person's lifelong collected information.
- It automatically collects important information that I experience.
- It automatically disburses important information for my thoughts, words, and deeds.

My visible body is temporary.

- It contains my soul, spirit, and heart.
- It contains my five physical senses and my total physical tent (bones, skin, blood, organs, hair, teeth, etc.).
- It will be replaced after my death with a spiritual body similar to what the Lord Jesus Christ had after His resurrection.

The Biblical Meaning of Heart

My personal realities (my own truths) gathered by my body, soul, and spirit are stored in my spiritual treasure chest, my heart. "For where your treasure is, there will your heart be also" (Matthew 6:21).

Of course, we are not talking about the physical heart that pumps blood. No, we are discussing spiritual matters. As we shall see from Jesus Christ's words about the heart, all of my life experience is stored in my deepest inner container called my heart. Yes, my heart holds what I think is actual truth, what is real to me.

My Heart Has Some Real Truth and Some False Truth

So of course, whenever actual truth, which is what God says, is in my heart, it blesses me greatly. However, every lie or misconception in my heart (anything that is not God's truth) causes me problems of some kind and makes me brokenhearted in some way. One of the great promises of the new covenant is that God provides a new heart as well as a new spirit. "I will give you a new heart and put a new spirit within you. I will take away your heart of stone and give you a heart of flesh" (Ezekiel 36:26 NLV).

One thing that Jesus did with the twelve disciples was to repair the brokenness in their hearts. His teaching replaced many lies with His truth. The church is to continue Jesus Christ's ministries. So, a ministry of mending broken hearts should be available whenever anyone's heartbrokenness becomes evident. Getting the lies and misconceptions replaced with what God says makes everything so much better in the end. Let us look at how this all works in more detail.

Jesus Christ said about human hearts, "From my heart come my thoughts, words, and deeds. Both good and bad come from my heart" (Luke 6:45; Matthew 15:18–19).

I get two points from Jesus's words. First, I collect both good and bad things in my heart, which become my reality. I believe these things to be solid, trustworthy facts. Jesus's second point is that my every thought, my every word, and my every action come from the reality which I stored in my heart. (That is the overflow process from my heart.)

Thoughts about Guarding a Heart

See how important the guarding of it is. You have seen mothers cover the eyes or ears of children. They are protecting those children's hearts from potential harm stored deep within. They are guarding those little hearts unknowingly. "Keep and guard your heart with all vigilance and above all that you guard, for out of it flow the springs of life" (Proverbs 4:23 AMP).

My heart is my inner container of my most important facts.

My human heart (the spiritual heart and not the physical organ) is my container (storage file) of my personal reality, my deepest believed conclusions, deductions, and facts (my life truths), all of which I have gathered through the functions of my body, soul, and spirit. These can also be generational blessings or curses (from my ancestors). Also, all new information that I automatically collect is added to my believed truth. This truth will be dispensed automatically, as I need it.

My heart also contains spiritual activity of both Holy Spirit and evil spirits.

My heart is also the home for the Holy Spirit (Ezekiel 36:27; 2 Corinthians 1:21–22; Galatians 4:6; 1 John 4:4). Besides God's forgiveness, the greatest new covenant provision is that the Holy Spirit of God is living within my own heart. The Holy Spirit is ready to put to death "my evil deeds within me" (Romans 8:13) and "pour in God truth" (Romans 5:5) within my heart and enable me to supernaturally obey all of God's laws (Ezekiel 36:27).

However, be aware that my heart also is my home for evil strongholds of lies, deceptions, curses, etc. This is why I must be careful about what goes into my heart from my eyes, ears, mouth, etc. (Acts 5:3; Mark 4:15; Luke 22:3; John 13:27)

Restatement

My believed reality is automatically stored in my heart.

My heart is the residence of the Holy Spirit, who is ready to put to death misdeeds and evil within me. Holy Spirit is ready to replace evil with God's truth.

The lies and false matters in my heart provide the place for evil-spirit strongholds of false beliefs, practices, doctrines, deceptions, curses, etc.

My heart also provides the automatic outflow of my believed truth, from which I think, speak, and behave, etc. (2 Corinthians 1:21–22; Galatians 4:6; Roman 5:5, 8:13, 7:17, 20; Acts 5:3, 9, 8:22–24).

Here is a story that explains the automatic steps of storing and outflow from one's heart.

The Black Pot

A two-year-old automatically stores his new realities into his heart.

A two-year-old reaches up and touches the black pot on Mama's stove. The child automatically collects his heart reality this way.

His body informs him, "Ouch, it hurts," from his touching finger.

His soul informs him, "The black pot hurts me," from his thoughts and emotions.

His spirit informs him, "No! It's wrong to touch the black pot," from his conscience.

The summary of his reality in his heart—The Black Pot Hurts Me.

The two-year-old overflows his words and actions from his heart reality.

Here is the rest of the story:

The Hidden Truth

The next day Mama tells the two-year-old to hand her the black pot. He looks up at the black pot, upset, says, "No," and refuses to hand it to Mama. Let's examine the automatic heart overflow process of the two-year-old.

The two-year-old thinks, speaks, and is disobedient, as the automatic overflow from his own belief within his heart reality says, "The black pot hurts me. I will not pick up the pot for you, Mommy."

The little boy did not know or understand that it is only a hot black pot that hurts, but he doesn't know that a black pot at normal temperature will not hurt him. He had not collected that real truth yet. Mama's duty becomes to teach him the truth about the effects of heat on the pot, especially the ones that make it harmful.

Every person in the world could correctly declare:

- My heart contains what I believe to be reality and truth.
- I do what I do because I believe what is in my heart.
- All people do what they do because they believe what is in their heart.
- There are things within everyone's heart that are not true.
- I should always look for real truth, which is a lot better.

Chapter 16: Gentle Restoration—God's Way to Wash Away Sin-Guilt

This tool has to do with a member of God's family who sins. These are the restoration processes to get right and stay right with God and man. Sin of every kind brings a separation of relationship with almighty God. Because He is holy, He expects His family to become and remain in a state of holiness and sanctification (being separated from sin and rightly related to our heavenly Father). These are spiritual steps by which the Holy Spirit of God brings inward changes.

Jesus Christ's New Covenant provides salvation from the lake of fire and cleansing to stay close to holy heavenly Father.

The Bible presents the necessities of every human being:

- To be saved from the eternal lake of fire, one must enter God's New Covenant available from the sin offering of the Lamb of God, Jesus Christ (Revelation 20:11–15; Ephesians 2:1–10; Hebrews 9:26–28).
- To keep the terms of the New Covenant, one must regularly be washed clean. The spiritually applied blood of the Lamb of God, Jesus Christ, is the cleanser (2 Timothy 2:21; Revelation 22:14; Matthew 18:15–22; John 13:6–17, 20:22–23; Galatians 6:1–10; Hebrews 9:14–15).

Three Primary Steps in the Restoration Process

Because of His love, God's restoration process is described in the three steps recorded in the book of Leviticus. Today (in New Testament times) these three steps are done spiritually and in the name of Jesus Christ. Jesus Christ's body and blood are the accepted sin offering to God.

"When anyone is guilty in any of these ways... he must confess in what way he has sinned and... as a penalty for the sin he has committed, he must bring to the Lord a sin offering and the priest shall make atonement for him for his sin" (Leviticus 5:5–6).

Step 1. The Person Must Confess Their Sin to God before a Witness

God's member of the New Covenant who is sanctified (any cleansed and prepared member of God's priesthood of believers) is authorized to hear the repentant confession of any child of God (one who is born again by the Spirit of God through the blood of the Lord Jesus Christ).

He or she is a witness to that person's:

- declaration of relationship through the Lord Jesus Christ as a member of God's spiritually reborn family within the New Covenant,
- earnest admission of the specific sin and deep repentance to flee and depart from it,
- full renouncement and removal of each and any symbol, hint, image, or token of that sin,
- desperate heart cry for God's forgiveness and complete cleansing through the precious blood of their personal Savior, our Lord Jesus Christ; and
- strong willingness to make full restitution if any is required by God's Word. (If restitution is necessary, all must agree upon the acceptable terms.)

Step 2: Each Person Must Present the Accepted Sin Offering to God

God's witness/worker accepts the person into membership in the New Covenant and assures the person of the worthy blood sacrifice of the Lord Jesus Christ, as received in heaven for God's legal requirement to be paid in full for this sin (Matthew 26:28; Hebrews 9:14–15).

Step 3: Each Person Shall Receive the Pronouncement of God's Forgiveness

God's witness/worker responds as an earthly agent for the Lord Jesus Christ, arranging for restitution if required. He or she has witnessed the obedience to God's holy Word and officially pronounced God's complete atonement, forgiveness and cleansing, over the one who had sinned (James 5:16; Galatians 6:1–2).

Normal Common Biblical Steps for Forgiveness between Family Members

These are normal commands and promises for establishing almighty God's forgiveness among His spiritual family. Each scripture that follows is a practical step that is important for every culture and every century of humanity: Matthew 18:15; Galatians 6:1–2; James 5:16; John 13:7–17; John 20:23; Hebrews 9:14–15, 10:22; Ezekiel 36:25–27.

Special Forgiveness Service Within a Church Family

What follows is a suggested format for a formal forgiveness ceremony designed to provide official evidence of forgiveness. Usually this is done whenever the committed sins affect a large number of the spiritual family, like the last steps of Matthew 18:17, 1 Corinthians 5:4–13, and 2 Corinthians 2:5–11.

A Gentle Restoration Service

"If your brother sins against you, go and show him his fault [that] every matter may be established by the testimony of two or three witnesses. Whatever you bind on earth will be bound in heaven, and whatever you loose on earth will be loosed in heaven. Where two or three come together in my name, there am I with them. How many times shall I forgive my brother when he sins against me? Jesus answered, 'I tell you, not seven times, but seventy-seven times'" (Matthew 18:15–22).

Begin an Open Discussion of the Biblical Background

Read these scriptures and answer all questions:

- Leviticus 5:5–10
- Proverbs 28:13
- Galatians 6:1–10
- 1 John 1:7
- 1 John 1:8–10
- James 5:16, 19–20
- Acts 19:17
- Hebrews 9:13–14
- 1 Peter 1:22–23

Provide God's Three Primary Steps for Biblical Restoration

1. The person must confess their sin to God before a witness. Discuss all pain inflicted on others by these sins.
2. The person must present the accepted sin offering to God. Make arrangements for any biblically required restitution or debt resolution.
3. The person shall receive the pronouncement of God's forgiveness

Document the Service

Ask each witness to God's official forgiveness in the Name of Jesus Christ to attach his or her name to the record.

Chapter 17: Mending Broken Hearts

The spiritually healthy worker in God's kingdom finds the correct keys to insert into a spiritual heart to open and fix it. We call this mending broken hearts. God's truth in my heart blesses me greatly. The contents of my heart that do not line up with God's truth cause me to be brokenhearted in those ways.

The Father planned for me to be in His system of identifying what is broken in my heart as well as becoming mended. For the remainder of my life journey, by using this tool correctly, I continue to learn what the Father has for me. This is the Kingdom of God's way of upgrading my understanding and knowledge continually.

What Jesus Christ Spoke about the Heart

- My heart is the container of my most treasured realities (Matthew 6:21).
- From my heart come my thoughts, words, and deeds (Luke 6:45; Matthew 15:18–19).
- I place evil in my heart through my lustful stares (Matthew 5:28).
- Jesus commands me to develop a gentle and humble heart like His (Matthew 11:29).
- It is into each one's own inner heart receptacle that God's Word is placed (Matthew 13:19).
- I can develop a gracious and good heart (Luke 8:15).
- I am wise to select and place forgiveness for others in my heart (Matthew 18:35).
- It is foolish to be slow to replace my realities with God's Word (Luke 24:25).
- I am like Jesus when I replace my heart troubles with God's Word (John 12:27).
- Jesus received peace instead of permitting His heart to be troubled (John 14:27).
- I intensify my relationship with God by keeping my heart pure (Matthew 5:8).
- Jesus healed the brokenhearted (Luke 4:18–19).

The writer of Proverbs says I must be on guard to keep God's truth in my heart:

"My son, pay attention to what I say; listen closely to my words. Do not let them out of your sight, keep them within your heart; for they are life to those, who find them and health to a man's whole body. Above all else, guard your heart, for it is the wellspring of life" (Proverbs 4:20–23).

How My Experiences, Thinking, and Actions Function

What I experience repeatedly through my own body, soul, and spirit functions become the deepest levels of my believed truth and reality. I store these facts, conclusions, and deductions in my heart, which becomes my inner reservoir/receptacle of experience. Next, my action-thought processes come from what I understand and believe to be true, which is stored within my heart.

Finally, my thoughts, words, actions and behaviors all come from my heart. My heart contains what I believe to be reality and truth. I do what I do because I believe what is in my heart. All people do what they do because they believe what is in their hearts.

The sinful fall of mankind resulted in heart damage.

This collection of terms from the Holy Bible describe various brokenhearted conditions: abominable, adulterous, afflicted, anguished, anxious, bitter, blighted, broken, callused, contrite, deceitful, deluded, despairing, evil, failed, fainted, faltering, fearful, filled with malice, grieving, grudging, hardened, haughty, heavy, in agony, lamenting, longing, lost, melted, murderous, obstinate, of stone, perverse, pierced, pounding, poured out, proud, sadden, sexually immoral, sick, slow, stolen, tormented, trembling, troubled, unbelieving, unrepentant, unyielding, wicked, withered and wounded.

Mending Broken Hearts

Almighty God does all heart mending. However, most often He uses New Covenant workers to gently write His words and His ways upon the wounded hearts (2 Corinthians 3:2–6).

In His hometown, our Lord, Jesus Christ read, "He hath sent me to heal the brokenhearted" and He also said, "This day is this Scripture fulfilled in your ears" (Luke 4:18–21 KJV; Isaiah 61:1–3 KJV).

Even though on that occasion in Nazareth He did not complete the reading of Isaiah 61:1–3, the story of Jesus's life demonstrates that He did mend the broken hearts of a handful of men who became a planting of the Lord to glorify God. Indeed, Christ's twelve disciples might well be called His oaks of righteousness.

In the King James Version, the phrase used in Isaiah 61:1 is "bind up the brokenhearted," although our Lord's reading in Luke 4:18 is "heal the brokenhearted." I choose this version, *mending the brokenhearted*.

The Greek word *katartizo* (Strong's NT: 2675) is used by both Matthew and Mark when they are describing that thing that anglers do, known as mending their nets. It is the labor of mending their nets that enables the net instrument to continue to be useful and by which an angler can continue to draw in his catch.

Mending seems the appropriate word to describe the repairing, putting in order, strengthening, and making one what he ought to be that actually is called for here. In the fishing occupation, the mended net is useful to catch fish. In the Kingdom of God, the mended hearts eventually result in a human orchard of "oaks of righteousness, a planting of the Lord for the display of his splendor" (Isaiah 61:3).

In this labor, usually some binding and healing are provided by the one who is mending the brokenhearted. We bind up the brokenhearted like a nurse gives aching limbs a gentle rubdown to bring them ease or as shattered bones and bleeding wounds are bound up so that they may knit and close again.

Those whose hearts are broken by sin either from their own lives or from others and are truly humbled under a sense of guilt and dread of wrath, are ready for heart mending.

The Lord Jesus described the heart ready for mending as belonging to those who are laboring, tired, weary, overburdened, heavy-laden, worn out, and burned out on religion (Matthew 11:28–30).

The replacement of deceptions and lies with God's appropriate truth and reality, when presented through agape love, brings peace and silences fear. This is one major path of soul rest which we call mending broken hearts (Jeremiah 6:16; Matthew 11:28).

Spiritual Families Do the Work of Mending

God sets the lonely in families (Psalm 68:6).

We must identify and deal with all problems. Difficult areas must be compensated for until the broken ways are replaced by healthy ways. The heart menders must provide mercy, grace, guidance, assistance, provision, and protection so wholeness can be achieved (Hebrews 12:12–17; James 5:16–20; Jude 22–25).

One's own human spirit can search the hidden deep parts of one's heart and reveal to one's mind the hidden essential information. The different causes of brokenness require different Kingdom of God truths. (Proverbs 20:27 KJV; Job 32:8; 1 Corinthians 2:10–11; 2 Timothy 2:15).

God gives some essential information by dreams and visions (Genesis 41:32, 46:2; 1 Samuel 3:10–11, 19; 1 Kings 3:5; Job 33:14–15, 29–30; Daniel 7:1; Matthew 27:19; Acts 2:17, 9:10–12, 10:3, 10, 17–19, 11:5, 16:9–10, 18:9, 26:19; 2 Corinthians 12:2–4; Revelation 1:10, 4:2, 17:3, 21:10).

Almighty God searches and reveals heart conditions by the Holy Spirit (Jeremiah 17:9–10; Matthew 13:11–12; John 14:26, 16:13–15; 1 John 2:20–21, 27; Romans 8:26–27; 1 Corinthians 12:7–11).

The heart mender suffers like a mother or dad suffers until the breaks are mended (Luke 22:44; 1 Corinthians 4:14; Galatians 4:19; Philippians 2:17; Colossians 1:24; Hebrews 5:7; Numbers 11:11–12; Isaiah 53:10–12).

The mender writes a spiritual word on broken hearts (1 Corinthians 9:1–2; 2 Corinthians 3:2–6, 12:14–15).

The mender loves the brokenhearted as no one else ever did (John 13:34–35; Romans 5:5).

The mender continues to express God's grace to the brokenhearted and finds God's ways to expose and remove the bitter roots (Hebrews 12:15).

Only God really knows what is in one's heart (Jeremiah 16:11–12, 17:9–10; Genesis 6:5, 8:20–21; Psalms 51:5, 53:2–3; Ecclesiastes 9:3; Matthew 15:19–20; Mark 7:20–23; Hebrews 3:12–13, 15; James 1:13–15, 4:1).

The Holy Spirit Uses Disciple Makers to Mend Broken Hearts

The Comforter is the Holy Spirit (Luke 11:13; John 14:16–17, 26).

The personality required of the mender includes being gentle, humble in heart, meek, and lowly in heart (Matthew 11:29, 12:20).

The mender must have within his own heart enough rest (i.e., relief, ease, refreshment, recreation, and blessed quiet for his soul) that the overflow can be placed into the brokenhearted one (Matthew 12:34–35; Romans 5:15, 15:13; Philippians 1:26; 1 Thessalonians 3:12).

The attitude of the mender must be like Christ, doing nothing out of selfish ambition or vain conceit, in humility considering others better than one's self, and looking not only to one's own interests but also to the interests of others (Philippians 2:1–10).

The mender himself must be mended. No one can give another what he does not possess. The one used in mending must first have had his or her own heart mended (Luke 6:40–42).

All of us have lies, misconceptions, deceptions, and false conclusions that we believe to be truth and reality. We need heart mending often (2 Timothy 2:20–26; 2 Peter 1:3–11).

God desires each of His children to know what His Word says on every subject. When the resulting pain in the believer's life causes him/her to cry out to the heavenly Father in anguish, God seeks to bring His truth into his/her heart, that will set that one free.

God sent His Son to heal broken hearts. We are agents to assist the Holy Spirit to mend broken hearts (Hebrews 12:13–16; 1 Corinthians 9:1–2; 2 Corinthians 3:2-6, 12:14–15).

Chapter 18: Endurance for Persecution

To be victorious when serious persecution comes, one must have previously developed endurance or perseverance in previous less difficult situations of life. Here are some Scripture passages that stress enduring in the faith of Jesus Christ.

- "All men will hate you because of me, but he who stands firm to the end will be saved" (Matthew 10:22).
- "Because of the increase of wickedness, the love of most will grow cold, but he who stands firm to the end will be saved" (Matthew 24:12–13).
- "And ye shall be hated of all *men* for my name's sake: but he that shall endure unto the end, the same shall be saved" (Mark 13:13 KJV).
- "He has reconciled you by Christ's physical body through death to present you holy in his sight, without blemish and free from accusation if you continue in your faith, established and firm, not moved from the hope held out in the gospel" (Colossians 1:22–23).
- "But Christ as a son over his own house; whose house are we, if we hold fast the confidence and the rejoicing of the hope firm unto the end" (Hebrews 3:6).
- "We desire that every one of you do shew the same diligence to the full assurance of hope unto the end: That ye be not slothful, but followers of them who through faith and patience inherit the promises" (Hebrews 6:11–12 KJV).
- "You need to persevere so that when you have done the will of God, you will receive what he has promised" (Hebrews 10:36).
- "The devil will put some of you in prison to test you, and you will suffer persecution for ten days. Be faithful, even to the point of death, and I will give you the crown of life" (Revelation 2:10).

More actions that assist me in difficult situations.

You and I know that living a totally sold-out life for King Jesus Christ is full of adventure and difficult circumstances. Yet, His powerful Holy Spirit is in my heart every step of my life journey (Galatians 4:6; 2 Corinthians 1:21–22). Below are some of the actions that assist me to persevere and endure in my faith until the difficulty is resolved.

I Pause and Consider the Negatives:

I recall the fearful thought that I could be a son of God in heaven with no rewards. "The fire will test the quality of each man's work. If what he has built survives, he will receive his reward. If it is burned up, he will suffer loss; he himself will be saved, but only as one escaping through the flames" (1 Corinthians 3:12–15).

Because I do not want those negative results, I shake myself and say, *I do not like that eternal situation.* My own firm statement encourages me to consider the positive.

I Pause and Consider the Positives:

His complete peace within me prevents all fears (Revelation 2:11, 20:6, 14–15, 21:8).

My food is specially prepared, and Jesus will whisper His special name to me, which is to be kept hidden on my gift stone (Revelation 2:7, 17, 3:12, 19:12; John 6:48–51, 57–58; Isaiah 56:5, 62:2).

My daily duty and position are patterned after those of King Jesus (Revelation 2:26–28, 3:21, 4:4, 10, 20:4, 6, 22:3–5, 16; Daniel 7:18, 22, 26–27; 2 Timothy 2:12; 2 Peter 1:19).

My Spirit-filled duty on earth will earn my white robe and secure name in the Book of Life while Jesus will see to it that the Father and His angels know how much I mean to Him (Revelation 3:5, 20:12, 21:27, 22:19; Exodus 17:14, 32:32–33; Deuteronomy 29:20; 2 Kings 14:27; Psalm 69:28; Matthew 10:32–33; Mark 8:38; 2 Timothy 2:12).

My position as a God-approved workman who rightly presents God's Word will earn me daily temple duty where I will always carry His three special name tags (2 Timothy 2:15; Galatians 2:9; Revelation 2:17, 3:12, 14:1, 22:4).

I will be found sitting on my throne like Jesus, telling all who will listen how I overcame just like He did (Matthew 19:28; Luke 22:28–30; Revelation 3:21, 4:4, 5:10, 20:6).

His forever inheritance gifts that I receive will be beyond description (Revelation 21:3–4, 7; Acts 20:32; Ephesians 1:13–14, 18; Colossians 1:12; 3:23–24; Hebrews 9:15; 1 Peter 1:3–6; Romans 8:14–17).

Under the King, I serve as a king among other kings. All will know me as a family member of the Most High (Daniel 2:44; 7:14, 18, 22, 26–27; Matthew 19:28, 25:31, 34; Luke 22:28–30; Romans 8:17; 1 Corinthians 6:2; 2 Timothy 2:12; 1 Peter 4:13, 5:1; Revelation 3:21, 4:4, 10, 11:15, 16, 20:4, 6, 22:3–5).

My earthly labors will earn full benefits (Revelation 20:12, 22:12; Job 34:11; Psalms 18:20, 62:12; Isaiah 40:10, 62:11; Jeremiah 17:10, 21:14, 32:19; Matthew 16:27, 25:21; Romans 2:6, 14:10–12; 1 Corinthians 3:8, 12–15; 2 Corinthians 5:10; Ephesians 6:7–8; Colossians 3:24–25).

I get first class treatment, since He put me in the Book of Life (Daniel 12:1; Malachi 3:16–18; Luke 10:20; Revelation 3:5, 20:12, 15, 21,27, 22:14).

His spiritual water is on tap forever, so I will never thirst again (Isaiah 44:3, 55:1; Jeremiah 2:13, 17:13; Zechariah 14:8; John 4:10, 7:37–38; Revelation 7:17, 21:6, 22:1, 17).

The Lord Jesus Christ is custom building my heavenly home (John 14:1–4; Revelation 2:7, 22:2, 14, 19).

Additional Comments

Good instructions include preparation for real difficulties to be faced. So, in His teaching, Jesus said, "I've told you all this so that trusting me, you will be unshakable and assured, deeply at peace. In this godless world, you will continue to experience difficulties. But take heart! I've conquered the world" (John 16:33 MSG).

These two pauses to reflect on God's word give me enough motivation to keep the faith and deny all fear within myself, no matter how great the required cost to me. Jesus Christ did this very same thing during times, calling for His own extreme obedience.

Jesus Christ's practice should be my own practice.

"Keep your eyes on Jesus, who both began and finished this race we're in. Study how he did it. Because he never lost sight of where he was headed—that exhilarating finish in and with God—he could put up with anything along the way: cross, shame, whatever. Now he is there, in the place of honor, right alongside God. When you find yourselves flagging in your faith, go over that story again, item by item, that long litany of hostility he plowed through. That will shoot adrenaline into your souls" (Hebrews 12:1–3 MSG).

Perseverance

In James 1:2-12, Jesus's half-brother provides specific steps to develop endurance (perseverance):

- "Consider it pure joy, my brothers and sisters, whenever you face trials of many kinds, because you know that the testing of your faith produces perseverance. Let perseverance finish its work so that you may be mature and complete, not lacking anything."
- "If any of you lacks wisdom, you should ask God, who gives generously to all without finding fault, and it will be given to you. But when you ask, you must believe and not doubt, because the one who doubts is like a wave of the sea, blown and tossed by the wind. That person should not expect to

receive anything from the Lord. Such a person is double-minded and unstable in all they do."
- "Believers in humble circumstances ought to take pride in their high position. But the rich should take pride in their humiliation—since they will pass away like a wildflower. For the sun rises with scorching heat and withers the plant; its blossom falls and its beauty is destroyed. In the same way, the rich will fade away even while they go about their business."
- "Blessed is the one who perseveres under trial because, having stood the test, that person will receive the crown of life that the Lord has promised to those who love him."

Chapter 19: Three Power Authorizations

Today's disciples of Jesus Christ can develop their own personal use of the three power authorizations that Jesus Christ gave His first disciples. Please see Part 5, Story #29—*Seven Hundred Students Experience Five Years of Peace and Excellence* and Story #30—*Thirteen Hundred Prisoners Enjoy the State's Most Peaceful Prison* for examples of this tool at work.

The three power authorizations are:

1. Preaching the Kingdom of God
2. Stopping all demonic activity
3. Confirmation of God's Miraculous Signs and Wonders

Brothers and sisters, please look at the amazing authority and power over the enemy that Jesus Christ gave to the apostles, the seventy-two others, the apostles' own people, and those who believe. In addition, realize that today (right now) you and I are in the same two categories of Christ's disciples as were the seventy-two others and those who believe. We are not the twelve apostles of Christ, but we are like the seventy-two others.

To the apostles, Jesus said: "He gave them power and authority to drive out all demons and to cure diseases, and he sent them out to preach the kingdom of God and to heal the sick so they set out and went from village to village, preaching the gospel and healing people everywhere (Luke 9:1–2, 6). "They went out and preached that people should repent. They drove out many demons and anointed many sick people with oil and healed them" (Mark 6:12–13).

To the seventy-two others, Jesus said, "The Lord appointed seventy-two others and sent them two by two. The seventy-two returned with joy and said, 'Lord, even the demons submit to us in your name.' He replied, 'I saw Satan fall like lightning from heaven. I have given you authority to trample on snakes and scorpions and to overcome all the power of the enemy; nothing will harm you'" (Luke 10:1, 17–20).

About the apostles' own people, God's Word says, on their release, Peter and John went back to their own people and reported ... they raised their voices together in prayer to God. "Sovereign Lord", Now, Lord, consider their threats and enable your servants to speak your word with great boldness. Stretch out your hand to heal and perform miraculous signs and wonders through the name of your holy servant Jesus. After they prayed, the place where they were meeting was shaken. And they were all filled with the Holy Spirit and spoke the word of God boldly (Acts 4:23–31).

About another group of God's people called "those who believe", the Word also says "And these signs will accompany those who believe: In my name they will drive out demons; they will pick up snakes with their hands; and when they drink deadly poison, it will not hurt them at all; they will place their hands on sick people, and they will get well ... The disciples went out and preached everywhere, and the Lord worked with them and confirmed his word by the signs that accompanied it" (Mark 16:15–20).

Preaching the Kingdom of God

The first authorization is to preach the kingdom of God. However, remember, I am not talking about you becoming a pastor, missionary, evangelist, etc. No, the truth is we each preach something in our present lives. We cannot escape our personal area of influence. Each of us has one. Do you have that understanding? Either you are fulfilling righteousness or unrighteousness. There is no escaping it. The way you live out your life does affect others.

Therefore, a more realistic way of speaking about this is to say that preaching the kingdom of God means that you only use words about the Kingdom of God if you have to. In truth, the way you live God's truth is your preaching. You must attempt to become the living Word of God yourself.

Your correct aim is attempting to be so much like Jesus that you demonstrate the truth and authority of Jesus Christ in your workplace. You see, today you have the opportunity and obligation to live out the words. Our workplace and homeplace actions do our preaching.

Your day-to-day authority does not come in preaching or saying words. No, your authority comes when you deliberately deny yourself and respond in the way Jesus Christ would at that given moment. In addition, you have already learned that you must be walking in soul rest and listening for the still, small voice of the Holy Spirit to do this. When your own Holy Spirit-led life obeys Jesus's commands and stands upon His promises and demonstrates His character traits to those around you, it brings significant results.

Paul said to think and do "whatever is true, whatever is noble, whatever is right, whatever is pure, whatever is lovely, whatever is admirable—if anything is excellent or praiseworthy" (Philippians 4:8).

Let us be sure that you get this point. You have Christ's authorization to be an example of the living Word of God wherever you are. You are to become like Jesus, who went about doing good. Christ expects you to do it through His Holy Spirit within you. The demons hope that you do not do it. The Holy Spirit and angels are ready to assist you so you can live out the Word of God daily.

Stopping All Demonic Activity

You have authorization to stop all demonic activity that comes as defense resistance to your presenting God's Word where you live and work. You should expect conflict from the Enemy, who does not want you to express God's love and truth. The hindering demonic activity will manifest itself in many ways. The fact is that most people around you do not want you to be "salt and light" or illustrate the love and Word of God. No, our fallen society, which ruled by the evil spirit prince of the world we live in, will raise up all kinds of obstruction.

Nevertheless, disciples of Christ learn that it is their duty to bring a halt to all such hindrances by using the authorization given to them in Jesus Christ's name. Usually your duty is not to cast out demons the way we read about Jesus doing it in demonized people. No, more frequently, it is bringing order, bringing peace, or bringing quietness to your circle of influence in the name of Jesus Christ.

In your home you stop the noisiness of the Enemy that is coming through your kids, your spouse, your neighbor, the TV, DVDs, radio, etc. His order, peace, and quietness come after you get these hindering things out of the way.

At work the people right next to you might be demonized people, but the fact is that you have the spiritual ability and authorization to cause that stuff to go away and fall to your side. In your little workspace or cubicle, you can still move and work in God's peace. During these situations you project the truth of God in your own surroundings. You stop the demonic from hindering you from living and preaching the truthful Word of God by exercising authorization.

Confirmation of God's Miraculous Signs and Wonders

Thirdly, you have authorization to ask almighty God for unusual confirmation about your life labor (lived-out truth). These are signs and wonders. A common result of this authorization will be people describing the peace, calmness, or excellence they have experienced. Start listening for their comments. Usually they do not know why they are saying these things. Sometimes this gives you a chance to explain your own source of success.

Something significant from your labor will have happened that affirmed notable results. These signs and wonders attract people's attention to what happened through you. Results of your successful work point to God without you saying anything about Him.

Jesus gives a job evaluation in Luke 10:1–2 and 10:16–18. Jesus said (in my own words), What you are thrilled about is just a part of your job description. I know you have authority over the demons. I know you can quiet down places. I know you can bring people and situations to order. These are the authorized tools that I have given you. But, do not rejoice about your tools. Instead, celebrate that you are in God's family by living out God's truth everywhere. Use your three power authorizations every day.

Chapter 20: Spiritual Warfare by the New Covenanters

God's family on earth is currently in a spiritual war with Satan. The total defeat and removal of Satan's power was completely accomplished by the death, burial, resurrection, and glorification of the Lord Jesus Christ. But the appointed day of Satan's eternal incarceration has not come yet. "Be strong in the Lord. For our struggle is not against flesh and blood, but against the rulers, the authorities, the powers of this dark world and the spiritual forces of evil" (Ephesians 6:10–13).

As a part of God's spiritual war force, we need to know God's ways and principles for us. Daily life takes on much more significance when I realize that I have a definite role in defeating the Enemy as I obey the Holy Spirit (1 Peter 2:4–5, 9; 2 Corinthians 3:4–6).

King Jesus Christ, who now has all power in heaven and on earth, continues His victorious ministry on earth through well-equipped, mature family members of almighty God. This spiritual warfare continues throughout the earthly journey of each member of God's family. God expects my daily life, lived in the power of the Holy Spirit, to bring defeat to the Enemy each day. It is by my simple obedience to the commandments of Jesus Christ while I am standing on His promises that I become a daily threat to the kingdom of darkness.

Making disciples is itself spiritual warfare. When we are doing excellent work as sons and daughters of almighty God, precious souls are being shown light in their darkness. Each person could be a valuable victory to be laid at the feet of our Lord, Jesus Christ. The body of the Lord Jesus Christ defeats Satan by bringing light and truth to our labors (Matthew 16:18–19).

Additional Scriptural Study

- The Lord God declared the war and the winner (Genesis 3:14–15).

- Evil spiritual forces use human beings as instruments against almighty God's family (Ephesians 6:10–13).
- Almighty God has set our war plan for the riddance of the devil (James 4:7; 1 Peter 5:8–11).
- We war as ministers of the New Covenant of the Spirit (2 Corinthians 3:4–6).
- We war as priests (1 Peter 2:4–5, 9).
- Jesus Christ is our High Priest (Hebrews 3:1, 5:7–10).
- Christ's Holy Spirit-led war force exercises authority (Luke 10:17–22).
- King Jesus watches our warfare (Luke 10:17–22).
- God's children have spiritual power to overcome every enemy scheme and never suffer spiritual harm (Luke 10:17–22).
- We must keep our relationship with Father and Son as the most important (Luke 10:17–22).
- Only those who humble themselves understand serious warfare matters (Luke 10:17–22).
- Our commander prays protection upon us (John 17:9–19).
- Deception and evil craftiness are tools of the enemy Serpent (Genesis 3:1).
- Religious people living unrepentant lives are grouped with the enemy Serpent (Matthew 3:7–8, 12:34–35, 23:33).
- Christ's war forces are to remove Satan's presence (John 12:30–31).
- King Jesus gives warfare information prior to battle (John 14:28–31).
- Battle victory comes from being free from sinful strongholds (John 14:28–31).
- Love of heavenly Father is proven by exact obedience (John 14:28–31).
- Like Jesus, we must be sent by God into spiritual conflict and not go on our own (John 8:42–48).
- Those who oppose God's kingdom do not understand His messenger (John 8:42–48).
- Our warfare is with those who are used by the Devil (John 8:42–48).

- Lying is from the Devil (John 8:42–48).
- His family understands God's truth, while those of the Enemy cannot (John 8:42–48).
- The one responding like Jesus is righteous (1 John 3:7–10).
- The one responding in an evil way is being used by the Devil (1 John 3:7–10).
- The purpose for Christ coming to earth was to wipe out enslavement to sin (1 John 3:7–10).
- The child of God keeps trying to stop his or her sinning and wants to stop it (1 John 3:7–10).
- A child of the Devil is content to continue in sin (1 John 3:7–10).
- A child of the Devil is content not to love a family member (1 John 3:7–10).
- Essential Christian truths must be held firmly (Romans 16:17–20).
- Christ's war force is to depart from selfish deceivers that use smooth talk and flattery (Romans 16:17–20).
- God will defeat His enemies that oppose Jesus's church (Romans 16:17–20).
- Christ's war force faces an enemy who has no power and authority (Colossians 2:13–15).
- Christ became the human sacrifice that demolished the Devil and his power of death (Hebrews 2:14–15).
- No child of God should be enslaved to fear (Hebrews 2:14–15).
- Christ is fully able to empower God's children to avoid sin (Hebrews 2:14–15).
- Christ's war force, which does not fear death, tell their Lamb's blood stories to overcome (Revelation 12:7–12).
- Praying against sin is essential (Luke 22:39–44).
- Christ's war force must do God's will (Luke 22:39–44)
- God hears prayers from "the reverent submissive" (Hebrews 5:7–10).
- Christ's war force is trained into maturity like Jesus was (Hebrews 5:7–10)

- Christ's warriors should use powerful spiritual gifts as weapons (Ephesians 4:7–10).
- Christ's war force has restoration provisions (1 John 2:1–2; Luke 22:31–32).
- The great commander knows ahead about our every battle (Revelation 2:8–3:20).
- The Holy Spirit places us in special places to be tempted by the Devil (Matthew 4:1).
- The Devil has the ability to take us places and show us what he wants to (Matthew 4:6–11).
- We have the power in Jesus's name to speak resistance to Satan (Matthew 4:6–11).
- Being full of the Holy Spirit does not prevent us from being tempted. The Devil's tempting may be a lengthy period (Luke 4:1–2).
- The Devil looks for opportune times to tempt God's children (Luke 4:13–15).
- When we defeat the Enemy in God's ways, we gain more power of the Holy Spirit (Luke 4:14).
- God permits the Devil's instruments to have power to tempt His children (John 19:8–11).
- By keeping ourselves pure and clean, the Enemy has no hold on us (John 14:28–31).
- Violating my conscience leads to crashing my faith (1 Timothy 1:18–19).
- God's war force must be holy and armed correctly (2 Corinthians 6:5–7).
- Spiritual weapons must be used (2 Corinthians 10:2–5).
- When evil comes, the full armor of God will protect completely (Ephesians 6:13–18).
- Spiritual strongholds can be overcome with God's truth (2 Corinthians 10:2–5).
- Deceit-filled, false ways are common (2 Corinthians 11:13–15).
- Many ministers deceive Christ's church (Matthew 24:4–5; Mark 13:5–6).

- Because of deceit, many turn from the faith (Matthew 24:10–13).
- Deceiving ministers with signs and miracles are common (Matthew 24:24–25).

"Submit yourselves to God. Resist the devil [and the devil] will flee from you" (1 Peter 5:8–11; James 4:7).

Jon Dean and Donna Smith

Chapter 21: God's Four-Step Health Plan

If I carefully listen to the Holy Spirit's instruction and if I diligently learn what God says is right and faithfully do it, if I constantly study and obey each of God's commands, and if I constantly keep the terms of God's covenant decrees, God will keep me healthy, take away all my sicknesses, and protect me from the common diseases of my community.

"He said, 'If you listen carefully to the Lord your God and do what is right in his eyes, if you pay attention to his commands and keep all his decrees, I will not bring on you any of the diseases I brought on the Egyptians, for I am the Lord, who heals you'" (Exodus 15:26).

Turning seventy-five years old this year (2014), my testimony is that my obedience to the previously outlined steps have brought to me God's health. I take no medications, have no impairments or medical conditions, and have been blessed with excellent health all of my life.

I have been with many ill people but never contracted illness. I stayed physically active and attempted to maintain balanced eating and resting routines. I badly broke my arm as a seventeen-year-old teenager and began to understand the Scripture passage, "Don't you know that you yourselves are God's temple and that God's Spirit lives in you? If anyone destroys God's temple, God will destroy him; for God's temple is sacred, and you are that temple" (1 Corinthians 3:16–17).

For more than fifty years I have carefully studied every Bible verse on sickness, illness, and healing. To me God's Word is very clear about this subject.

Please ask heavenly Father to reveal his truths about healing to you in these important scriptures:

Three very significant passages on this subject are Job 33:14, 19–30, 1 Corinthians 11:28–31, and Revelation 2:21–23. Jesus Christ's record of healings show categories of sickness and illness that we have today. His actions provide for us examples to follow, as we are guided by the Holy Spirit.

- Some illnesses are because of the sins of our parents.
- Some illnesses are because of the sins of those we are around.
- Some illnesses are because of our own sins.
- Some illnesses purpose to bring God glory.
- Most illnesses among God's family are to get one's attention to bring correction and wisdom.

Almighty God taught me a great lesson from a lengthy illness. He got my attention. You can read this true-life testimony in *Part 5, Story #13–Instant Healing from Twenty Years of Allergies.*

What follows next is a testimony about health from co-author, Donna Smith. Please ask heavenly Father to provide you with great revelations. See how she gives God great glory.

Donna Smith's Health Testimony

JD and I have been married fifty-two years (2014). While he has walked in good health during these years, I have had twelve surgeries and suffered the effects of Parkinson's and scoliosis. I wanted to be healed and I had the church elders pray for me and welcomed the prayers of many (2 Corinthians 1:11).

In 2007, JD and I took a year's sabbatical from ministry, sold most of our furniture, leased our house, and rented an apartment in Ft. Worth. It was a wonderful year of sharing many things and a lot of praying and Bible study along with much fun and relaxation.

As JD guided me through every Scripture passage in the Bible on healing, I couldn't ignore how many times God used illness to get the attention of His people to examine themselves for sin in their lives. Like with them, God wants to humble and test me to see what is in my heart (Deuteronomy 8:2).

During that time God revealed to me that many of my responses to previous life events were sinful in God's eyes. I had many unconfessed sins in my life. For example, I was selfish, prideful, jealous, deceitful, and full of vanity. I was more fearful of people's displeasure than God's displeasure. This story is about my vanity and pride.

It was the beginning of a new school year, and all of the teaching staff met at the high school auditorium (several hundred people). The motivational speaker asked all in the audience to stand. I was sitting with some fellow teachers in the back of the room and had on a red dress. The speaker began stating some conditions and instructed us to sit down when we couldn't meet the stated condition. He asked, "Do you smoke more than a pack a day? Do you drink more than three cokes a day?" among other things. People would begin to sit down. "Do you always wear a helmet when you ride a bike?" I thought, *Even though I don't have a bike, I would wear a helmet if I did.* I continued to stand. Finally, I was the only one standing. The speaker made some funny statement about the woman in the red dress. I finally sat down. Later as I thought about the event, I was horrified at what I had done. I was selfish, full of pride, and I had lied.

Another trying time for our family was the seven-year period when I was anorexic (1978–1985). I began playing tennis and lost a few pounds. I felt really good about myself and decided to try to lose some more. As I lost weight, I became obsessed with being thin. I would eat very little and exercised excessively. Before long I weighed in at ninety-eight pounds. Everyone was telling me how bad I looked; however, all I could see was how thin I was, and I loved it.

My family got tired of putting up with my strict eating regulations. It was no fun for us to go out to eat because I would complain about the food and most times just wouldn't eat.

I can't explain how I was set free. I began to eat a little more and realized I could play tennis better if I were stronger. God just opened my eyes to see the damage I was doing to my body and family. It took about a year for me to be set free from the disorder, but I praise God for His mercy and grace in bringing me back to the truth.

As the Holy Spirit brought each sinful incident to my mind, I confessed it to God in front of JD. I would weep and grieve over the pain that I had caused friends, teachers, and family members. When appropriate, I would confess to the person who was involved in that event. I realized the wonderful truth that confessing my sins to God in the presence of another person set me free. Now full of God's forgiveness, I gladly share God's grace and mercy, which fills my life.

Thank God He delivered me by the blood of Christ, who through the eternal Spirit offered Himself unblemished to God and cleansed my conscience from acts that lead to death so that I may serve the living God (Hebrews 9:13–14). I wasn't healed physically but spiritually. I was free of guilt. My conscience had been cleansed by the blood of Christ (Hebrews 9:11–16).

I am spiritually healthier than I was two years ago. Physically the doctors tell me that I am an inspiration to them and stress the importance of my continuing the exercises and following God's directions.

"Why art thou cast down, O my soul? And why art thou disquieted within me? Hope thou in God, for I shall yet praise Him, who is the health of my countenance and my God" (Psalm 42:11).

Job would not listen to God's messenger, who identified Job's sins that Satan's testing exposed. I thank almighty God for sending JD, my personal Elihu. Together we fall on our knees in thanksgiving for understanding what God has done in my life (Job 33:14, 19–30). I now see God's smile and celebrate at finding myself right with God. For God's praise I sing and play my piano every time I can as my testimony. I messed up my life, and it wasn't worth it. But God stepped in and saved me from certain death. I'm powerfully alive now. Once more I see the light (Job 33:19–30).

2019 Update:

Five years have passed with God's Four-Step Health Plan, continuing. We all know that everyone will experience death, when almighty God approves of it; for me (Jon Dean), it appears to be within one year.

In June of 2018, my physicians discovered cancer in my body verified with biopsies. Because there were no symptoms, we were quite surprised. After serious prayer, I chose not to have the suggested surgeries and treatments. Now we realize what a blessing this notice has been, for the preparation of our spiritual team and earthly family. Of course, we all know that only almighty God knows these things. In December of this year, I will finish 80 amazing, wonderful years from God. The psalmist had written, "The length of our days is seventy years—or eighty, if we have the strength" Psalms 90:10).

During this year several have asked me something like this, "Why are you so happy, almost jubilant at the news of your life ending?" I really look forward to meeting the heavenly Father, Lord Jesus Christ and Holy Spirit, as they truly are. I also see that I am blessed like many of God's sons.

Blessed like Hezekiah:

"In those days was Hezekiah sick unto death. And the prophet Isaiah the son of Amoz came to him, and said unto him, Thus saith the LORD, Set thine house in order; for thou shalt die, and not live" (2 Kings 20:1–11).

Blessed like Peter:

"I know that I'm to die soon; the Master has made that quite clear to me" (2 Peter 1:14 MSG).

Blessed like Paul:

"For I am already being poured out like a drink offering, and the time for my departure is near. I have fought the good fight, I have finished the race, I have kept the faith. Now there is in store for me the crown of righteousness, which the Lord, the righteous Judge, will award to me on that day—and not only to me, but also to all who have longed for his appearing" (2 Timothy 4:6–8).

This is my latest update about how almighty God is concluding His health plan in my life. Donna and I think His plan is marvelous.

Chapter 22: Learning to Love the Fear of God

We thank our Father for causing us to delight in the fear of the Lord. While it sounds strange to delight in or enjoy the fear of the Lord, I will attempt to explain it to you.

It was my surprise at age sixteen to be offered a job by a senior manager of a successful store chain in Dallas, Texas. While many of my co-workers expressed discomfort and anxiety toward this senior executive, it was my joy to always obey his instructions and carefully comply with each company policy. I enjoyed the opportunity to work hard for a well-organized supervisor who always dealt truthfully. Because of the stores sequential processes, I advanced rapidly through each position. Soon for a good salary, I worked as much as I wanted to during holiday and summers. Eventually, I became an on-call salesmen for several stores in the chain.

I discovered that almighty God is the ultimate well-organized senior executive who always deals through truth. My fear would be from my being ignorant or insensitive to His instructions that would disappoint my heavenly Father. Here are my favorite passages on this subject:

"For as high as the heavens are above the earth, so great is his love for those who fear him. As a father has compassion on his children, so the LORD has compassion on those who fear him" (Psalm 103:11, 13).

"Therefore, my dear friends, as you have always obeyed—not only in my presence, but now much more in my absence—continue to work out your salvation with fear and trembling" (Philippians 2:12).

"Since you call on a Father who judges each person's work impartially, live out your time as foreigners here in reverent fear" (1 Peter 1:17).

"Show proper respect to everyone, love the family of believers, fear God, honor the emperor. Slaves, in reverent fear of God submit yourselves to your masters, not only to those who are good and considerate, but also to those who are harsh" (1 Peter 2:17–18).

Chapter 23: Perfect Peace from the Prince of Peace

On many occasions, when I directed the anxious (worried, distraught, frightened, scared) person to put his or her mind upon something better, they came into amazing, powerful peace. Our wise disciples use this tool often.

Applying the steps outlined by the apostle (Philippians 4:8–9) releases the perfect peace from Jesus Christ, the Prince of Peace.

"Do not be anxious about anything, whatever is true, whatever is noble, whatever is right, whatever is pure, whatever is lovely, whatever is admirable—if anything is excellent or praiseworthy—think about such things. And the God of peace will be with you" (Philippians 4:6–9).

"You will keep in perfect peace those whose minds are steadfast, because they trust in you" (Isaiah 26:3).

"For to us a child is born, to us a son is given, and the government will be on his shoulders. And he will be called Wonderful Counselor, Mighty God, Everlasting Father, Prince of Peace" (Isaiah 9:6).

Chapter 24: What We Gain by Giving Up Everything To Follow Jesus Christ

In June 2019, I received notice from my physicians that I had less than one year to live, yet Donna and I remain happy in the Lord and enjoy daily Soul Rest. Since 1969, Jesus Christ's commands in Matthew 6:19–24, are our day-to-day decision guide to lay up eternal treasure instead of accumulating earthly stuff. Recently, my beloved wife Donna counted the houses we left to obey Lord Jesus, listed the occupations/businesses we left, and named family and friends from whom we separated.

"And everyone who has left houses or brothers or sisters or father or mother or wife or children or fields for my sake will receive a hundred times as much and will inherit eternal life. But many who are first will be last, and many who are last will be first" (Matthew 19:29–30).

Please be greatly encouraged as you discover what is gained:

Jesus said, "In the same way, those of you who do not give up everything you have cannot be my disciples" (Luke 14:33; also Mark 10:21, 28; Luke 5:11, 28).

We have given up everything for Christ and our deliberate plan is to "keep the terms of the New Covenant" through Holy Spirit's power until our death. Here are some of our rewards:

TO POSSESS THE KINGDOM FOREVER: "But the holy people of the Most High will receive the kingdom and will possess it forever…the sovereignty, power and greatness of all the kingdoms under heaven will be handed over to the holy people of the Most High" (Daniel 7:18–27).

TO RECEIVE MORE THAN WE GAVE UP: "And everyone who has left houses or brothers or sisters or father or mother or children or fields for my sake, will receive a hundred times as much and will inherit eternal life" (Matthew 19:27–29).

TO SERVE CHRIST IN OUR PREPARED KINGDOMS: "Then the King will say 'Come, you who are blessed by my Father; take your inheritance, the kingdom prepared for you since the creation of the world" (Matthew 25:31–46).

TO RECEIVE THE KINGDOM OUR FATHER IS PLEASED TO GIVE US: "Do not be afraid, little flock, for your Father has been pleased to give you the kingdom" (Luke 12:32).

TO RECEIVE AN UNSHAKABLE KINGDOM: "Therefore, since we are receiving a kingdom that cannot be shaken, let us be thankful, and so worship God acceptably with reverence and awe" (Hebrews 12:28).

TO TAKE CHARGE OF TEN CITIES: "Well done, my good servant!' his master replied. 'Because you have been trustworthy in a very small matter, take charge of ten cities" (Luke 19:17).

TO RECEIVE MANY NATIONS: "Ask me, and I will make the nations your inheritance, the ends of the earth your possession" (Psalm 2:8).

TO SIT WITH KING JESUS: "To the one who is victorious, I will give the right to sit with me on my throne, just as I was victorious and sat down with my Father on his throne" (Revelation 3:21).

TO REIGN ON THE EARTH: "You have made them to be a kingdom and priests to serve our God, and they will reign on the earth" (Revelation 5:10).

TO RECEIVE AUTHORITY TO JUDGE AND REIGN: "I saw thrones on which were seated those who had been given authority to judge. They came to life and reigned with Christ a thousand years. They will be priests of God and of Christ and will reign with him for a thousand years" (Revelation 20:4–6).

TO BECOME KINGS IN THE NEW EARTH: "The nations will walk by its light, and the kings of the earth will bring their splendor into it" (Revelation 21:24).

TO REIGN FOREVER: "There will be no more night. They will not need the light of a lamp or the light of the sun, for the Lord God will give them light. And they will reign for ever and ever" (Revelation 22:5).

Part Five: Our Eyewitness Testimony – Some of God's Amazing Deeds on Our Journey

It is God's plan that members of His spiritual family collect and share their personal stories about God with the next generation (Psalm 78:1–8). You also gain amazing power over Satan's temptations when you recall the true-life testimonies of almighty God's past care of you and your family (Revelation 12:10–11). We encourage you to write down your own stories of God's action in your life journey, to be handed to others.

My report from the late 1930's until 1961, is that I was greatly blessed by parents who provided me a lifestyle of serving almighty God and sharing with others. But you are reading our report which began in 1961, when heavenly Father brought Donna Louise Williams and me into courtship, resulting in our 1962 marriage.

It is our great joy and honor to report to you that heavenly Father always kept His promises and made daily provisions available for our family. We never did without life essentials and usually were able to bless those around us. But just as important has been the development of our inward joy and consistent peace from heavenly Father, which we find difficult to limit to a few words. Basically, there is nothing that happens that ever removes us from heavenly Father's all-powerful love.

And in the overall, big scheme of things, Jesus Christ's familiar prayer phrases, "Thy kingdom come, Thy will be done on Earth as it is in heaven" is what almighty God has brought to pass in our lives.

Here are a few stories, requested by our disciple friends that demonstrate the amazing, real-life, eye-witness accounts of supernatural Creator God interacting in our day to day lives. In each story, enjoy the honor and glory that heavenly Father brought to Himself.

Finally, be greatly encouraged to receive and report to others, God's ever-expanding signs and wonder eye-witness reports from your journey.

Stories Listed by Categories

Please enjoy reading some of our stories about almighty God's wonderful care and provision for our family since 1962. Most of these dramatic events were witnessed by our children and coworkers, who joined us in giving thanksgiving to almighty God. We have informally categorized these stories by their content:

Dreams/Visions: #8, #9, #18

Evangelism: #4, #23, #24, #29

Finances: #1, #15, #21, #25

Healing: #13, #18

Prayer Results: #2, #5, #7, #11, #15, #16, #28

Property: #5, #11, #22, #23

Protection: #18, #19, #20, #24

Spiritual Warfare: #3, #6, #10, #12, #17, #19, #20, #22, #26, #27

Vehicles: #7, #9, #28

Work Solutions: #9, #14, #16, #21, #23

Story # 1–Banker Sees God's Provisions

In 1994, the financial climate of our town was very depressed. The public was not buying nonessential items. Nevertheless, almighty God knew it was time for our business to sell and He brought a buyer. A family from the panhandle of Texas came to me and wanted to buy Smith's Music Place. They did not purchase our commercial building, but they did buy the music business itself, which was a great blessing.

At that point we decided to rent our commercial building, which needed $10,000.00 of repair work. I arranged for a local signature note from our banker since my prayer results had brought no income. On the day I was to sign the note at his desk, we were interrupted by a telephone call from my daughter. "Dad, you'd better come home and see what came in the mail", she said with a chuckle.

When I delayed signing the note and excused myself from the banker, he said, "JD, have you been praying again?" Sure enough, the amazing hand of God was present once more. In the mail was a cashier's check to me for $10,000.00. We had no idea or expectation that this would be coming as a timely portion of an inheritance from a distant relative. This was God's provision.

After we thanked God on our knees at the house, I returned to the bank where the longtime banker friend and I thanked the Lord Jesus Christ.

Story #2 – Broom Closet Prayer

At church I served as senior high Bible teacher, ordained deacon, interim minister of music, and a member of the pulpit committee. After approximately five years I became burdened for many within the church. I could see that it was life's common problems that prevented most folks from maturing in their faith and fulfilling God's will in their lives. As I discussed this with older Christians, including my senior pastors, no one had any answers. In fact, it appeared to me that something was lacking in Christianity as we experienced it.

One Wednesday night before the service, I was so burdened that I went in a church broom closet and cried out in prayer to God, "Dear heavenly Father, there are so many precious people who are hurting spiritually and physically with no lasting help offered. We church leaders are doing all we know to do, but there has to be more. The New Testament things we read about just do not happen in our church life. I cannot go on this way. Please, Lord, show me what is missing, and I will share it with my friends in our town. In Jesus Christ's name, amen."

Then our heavenly Father took us for a seven-year training program by moving us to five other cities. At the end of seven years the Lord returned us to the same town with a much deeper understanding of the Kingdom of God. God's word presents how He changes people and nations.

These disruptions within human hearts, we now call God's Six-step Change Plan from Jeremiah 1:10 and 24:6–7.

1. Uproot—painful uncovering of lies, deceptions, false beliefs, and the counterfeit.
2. Tear down—sever, chop off at roots, cut down, stop relationships.
3. Destroy—crush, dismantle, rip to pieces.
4. Overthrow— remove, separate from, get rid of completely.
5. Build—replace low things (evil) with right things (righteous).
6. Plant—introduce truth, wisdom, knowledge, and understanding.

God's Six-step Change Plan has produced over forty-five years of advancing the Kingdom of God throughout the world, which is partially revealed within these pages.

Story #3 – "Daddy, Help Me Get Rid of This Power That Makes Me Do Evil"

The parents of their sixteen-year-old daughter were very distraught and said to us, "She has never done anything like this before—lying, sneaking out to meet this boy, not caring about school rules and family responsibilities. Our discipline does not work, nor our pleading. It is just not like her. Please help us."

When we learned that the child's biological mother had been very wild at this age and that no spiritual restoration had occurred, we suggested that spiritual warfare was in order. We considered the biblical steps of victory over generational and unresolved bitter roots.

Up to this time this family did not know about demons or spiritual warfare. The parents began following our instructions and using suggested prayers in the name of Jesus Christ each morning and evening (1 Peter 5:8–9; 2 Timothy 2:20–26).

What a joy it was when the daughter said about two weeks later, "Daddy, help me get rid of this power that makes me do evil."

She and her parents began learning about spiritual warfare and were faithful to keep themselves clean spiritually. She completed high school and college, and she is now the wife and mother in the home of a successful minister.

Story #4–"Come to my camp, Smitty! You're a priestee man, aren't you?"

Cadillac Jones was a skilled welder and highly in demand by oil-wealthy ranchers for constructing corrals, holding pens, chutes, and barns. He was also known as the best barbed wire fence man anywhere, with a mustang-like wild character. The old-west cowboy-like fellow was proud that he did not like people and had not been in a town in seven years.

Cadillac let everyone know that he was a confirmed functioning alcoholic who required each rancher to get his weekly grocery and liquor list delivered on time to his campsite, a twenty-square-foot military tent anchored to his eighteen foot Airstream RV, which covered his WWII Jeep, and a boiling coffeepot over the campfire.

For about six weeks, two ranch hands and I (the foreman) joined Cadillac six days a week to construct a barbed wire perimeter around a new planting field. One cold winter Saturday afternoon we were closing up early because snow was falling. Cadillac turned to me and said, "Come to my camp, Smitty! I want to talk with you. You're a priestee man, aren't you?"

Well, I was somewhat concerned, not knowing just how to answer him. If I said, "No," it would be a lie to God, but on the other hand, if I said, "Yes," Cadillac might cause me some kind of serious concern. As the snow fell, I went inside his RV and drank coffee while Cadillac had something stronger. It turned out that we had a serious talk about many things, mostly about hypocritical Christians fussing and competing over church membership. Most importantly, he begged Jesus Christ to be his personal Savior into heaven.

On the way home the Holy Spirit whispered to my spirit, "Well done, JD. Your honest work life was respected by this precious man and opened the door of his heart for important things. This timing was very important in Cadillac's life."

About four months later he came to my home with more questions about Jesus Christ. Two months after that I read the newspaper account of his obituary.

Story #5– Estate Finances Provided

As executor of my father's will, I (Donna) was well aware of the need for more funds to provide for my mother's nursing home care. The main asset we had was my parents' home. Our son lived there while he attended college and several of his friends rented the extra bedrooms. When the boys made other living arrangements, we put the house on the market. Our realtor had been in the high school choir under JD's direction. It was fun working with her and we fully expected the house to sell rapidly.

Weeks went by, and I was disappointed that we had not heard from Mary, our realtor. When she did call a few days later, she informed me that the market was flooded with houses like ours and about the same price range. It was not very encouraging. She suggested having an open house, which we did, but with no positive results.

We knew that God was our source, not a house sale. The house was just a tool. We prayed for God to provide for our needs and put our trust in Him. At Mary's next call, she told of showing a man houses that fit his needs. However, when they passed our house, the man said he would like to look at it. She explained that it was not what he was looking for according to his own specifications, but he insisted on seeing the house. Once in, he said it was exactly what he wanted and agreed to our asking price and paid cash.

Story #6– Great Stories of Gentle Restoration

The New Covenant Provides High Priest Jesus Christ at God's Right Hand

"…Jesus has become the guarantor of a better covenant…because Jesus lives forever, he has a permanent priesthood… he is able to save completely those who come to God through him, because he always lives to intercede for them. Such a high priest truly meets our need— one who is holy, blameless, pure, set apart from sinners, exalted above the heavens…since we have a great priest over the house of God, let us draw near to God with a sincere heart and with the full assurance that faith brings, having our hearts sprinkled to cleanse us from a guilty conscience and having our bodies washed with pure water" (Hebrews 7:22–28, 10:21–23).

The Lord Jesus Taught His Apostles to Spiritually Wash Each Other

Jesus Christ demonstrated how to witness a person's repentant sin confession and then pronounce God's forgiveness. "Again Jesus said, As the Father has sent me, I am sending you. Receive the Holy Spirit. If you forgive anyone's sins, their sins are forgiven; if you do not forgive them, they are not forgiven" (John 20:21–23). "Jesus replied…Now that I, your Lord and Teacher, have washed your feet, you also should wash one another's feet. I have set you an example that you should do as I have done for you." (John 13:7–15)

All Sin Must Be Confessed and Forgiven

Lord Jesus Christ said, "If your brother or sister sins, go and point out their fault. If they listen to you, you have won them over. But if they will not listen, take one or two…so that 'every matter may be established by the testimony of two or three witnesses." Truly I tell you, whatever you bind on earth will be bound in heaven, and whatever you loose on earth will be loosed in heaven. If two of you on earth agree, it will be done for them by my Father in heaven. For where two or three gathered in my name, there am I with them. Peter asked, "Lord, how many times shall I forgive my brother or sister who sins against me? Up to seven times?" Jesus answered, "I tell you, not seven times, but seventy-seven times" (Matthew 18:15–22).

The Apostle Paul said, "Brothers and sisters, if someone is caught in a sin, you who live by the Spirit should restore that person gently. But watch yourselves, or you also may be tempted. Carry each other's burdens, and in this way you will fulfill the law of Christ. Therefore, as we have opportunity, let us do good to all people, especially to those who belong to the family of believers" (Galatians 6:1–10).

At times a Gentle Restoration Service is required.

Gentle Restoration Service Example #1

The college student daughter of a church leader informed her parents that she is guilty and ashamed for her sexual sin which has resulted in her pregnancy by a nonbeliever. The parents and daughter shared these matters with the church leadership, who offered the family a Gentle Restoration Service (Galatians 6:1–10) since this sin affected the church family. The results brought amazing blessings to the church family. As the word spread, other churches asked for Bible explanations and applications, which introduced Gentle Restoration Services in many additional locations.

Gentle Restoration Service Example #2

When a veteran minister who had been fired by one local church for sexual immorality, appealed to the leadership of a neighbor-church for Gentle Restoration, the church leadership asked its membership to prayerfully consider joining the restoration team to assist in this lengthy process.

With oversight by church elders, a team of eight senior men and women wisely and carefully proceeded to administer day and night oversight and protection for this serious, repentant man. Great joy was expressed when three years later, this gently restored minister was reinstated in leadership in another church.

Gentle Restoration Service Example #3

A 70-year-old church member, who worked at the church needed three hundred dollars unexpectedly. Too prideful to tell anyone about his financial need, he pawned one hundred unused church chairs, planning to get them out of hock before anyone missed them. However, a church member recognized the chairs in the pawn shop and told the church leadership of this apparent theft of church property. A Gentle Restoration Service *(described in Chapter 16)* provided the return of property and biblical restitution with no legal charges being filed. The correct results from applying 1 Corinthians 6:1–12 and Galatians 6:1–10 quietly spread in the town and abroad. The church leadership obeyed the word of God and brought great glory to almighty God.

When Correction by the Church is Refused

"If your brother or sister sins, go and point out their fault. If they still refuse to listen, tell it to the church; and if they refuse to listen even to the church, treat them as you would a pagan or a tax collector" (Matthew 18:15–22). Continue in prayer for these to come to their senses and return to the family of God. See Luke 15:11–32 for the correct attitude to exhibit towards these precious brothers and sisters. See also: 1 Corinthians 5:1–11, 6:9–11; 2 Corinthians 2:5–11.

Story #7– Go to the Bar for Help

When a relative passed away in a rest home out of state, an amazing series of events took place concerning her final arrangements. In March, a rare ice storm covered the area. When I arrived at the airport in the midst of falling sleet, ground traffic was almost at a standstill. From that city I was to transport the son of the deceased and his mother's body to the burial city. Under normal driving conditions this would be approximately a four-hour drive.

The airfreight transfer vehicles were grounded because of the bad weather, preventing me from picking up the casket in a normal fashion. I excused myself from my passenger and had a prayer. Then I made a phone call to the airfreight office for an alternative pickup.

After I explained my difficulty with weather and time restraints for the long drive to the funeral home, the airfreight terminal supervisor provided a special permission pass. With flashers glaring, I slowly drove the mile in falling sleet to the terminal, completed my pickup, and picked up my passenger at the baggage area.

Two and a half hours later while I had stopped for refueling, my ice-covered van would not start. During the falling sleet I discovered that the distributor rotor cap was cracked. It was 5:30 p.m. on Friday afternoon. After serious prayer the answer came. "Go to the bar directly next to the service station and seek to contact a local repairman."

In faith and obedience, I did so. To my great joy, God brought an amazing solution. A man sitting at the bar overheard my explanation to the barkeeper and said, "Come with me to my pickup." Then in the rain he reached into his toolbox, got the exact replacement part, and handed it to me, saying, "I don't want a penny for it. I appreciate what you are doing for the family."

As my passenger returned from his restroom break in the service station, I closed the engine cover after replacing the part, and the van started immediately. With slow and careful driving, we made our destination without further events. Only God could have made that happen.

Story #8– God's Dishwasher

This was a night dream. While I was washing dishes in the basement of a large restaurant, the trays, glasses, dishes, and silverware all came to me down a conveyor belt. My job was to make clean and ready every type of cooking and serving vessel used in this full-service restaurant.

After I washed each item, I would examine them to make sure they were thoroughly clean with no residue, smudges, or fingerprints. At times a pot or pan would need its shape restored by pressure from a wooden spoon, which took more effort. Each item had to pass the crystal clean examination I gave before it was placed on a cart. Someone else took the cart of clean vessels to their proper place for service.

At times when nothing came down the conveyor belt, I asked for additional work so that I might feel that I was earning my salary. The manager responded, "JD, I need you to be ready at all times to clean and make my vessels ready for my use."

Later the Holy Spirit gave me these interpretations and applications:

The restaurant manager represented the Lord Jesus Christ, giving me directions.

The restaurant represented the local churches where I met God's workers.

Each vessel represented any worker serving in God's churches.

The conveyor belt represented the various ways Jesus workers came to me.

The dishwashing represented the restoration and equipping of Jesus's workers.

Since the early 1980's many workers from different denominations came into my life seeking counsel for themselves and their churches. From ten years of assisting six state prison chaplains develop discipleship programs, ministers in the free world began contacting me. One county ministerial alliance hosted my two-hour weekly share time for a year, which provided many individual breakfasts and lunch follow-up times.

Several local church leadership teams asked for training in mending hearts and gentle restoration. At the time of this publication (2014), it continues to be my joy to serve God's vessel-workers both locally and in other nations. I attempt to follow the Apostle Paul's instructions, when speaking of Lord Jesus Christ, he said, "He is the one we proclaim, admonishing and teaching everyone with all wisdom, so that we may present everyone fully mature in Christ. To this end I strenuously contend with all the energy Christ so powerfully works in me" (Colossians 1:28–29).

A friend has said, "You are God's Dishwasher when you teach us how to be useful to the Master and prepared for any good work."

"Do your best to present yourself to God as one approved, a worker who does not need to be ashamed and who correctly handles the word of truth. In a large house there are articles not only of gold and silver, but also of wood and clay; some are for special purposes and some for common use. Those who cleanse themselves from the latter will be instruments for special purposes, made holy, useful to the Master and prepared to do any good work" (2 Timothy 2:15–21).

Story #9– God's Mechanical Repair Shop

When puzzled by my failure with the written instructions to rebuild a carburetor, I asked for the Lord's help in Jesus Christ's name. When no answer came, I quieted my soul and began working on the vehicle's rear brakes. In the midst of removing a brake spring, a still, small voice spoke information about a carburetor adjustment. At first, I rejected the information, determined to keep my mind on the brake job before me. Then that familiar voice got my attention. This was the answer to my previous prayer.

I stopped the brake work and made the specific adjustment on the carburetor according to what I had received from the still, small voice. As I rechecked the written directions and found nothing about this adjustment, I rejoiced and thanked our Lord for His provision of truth. Next I experienced the great sound of a quickly starting engine that performed well. God did it again. Sometime later, God had us operate Smith's Auto Repair for several years.

Story #10–Good Men and Women Blinded by Satan, the Enemy

The subject at the county ministerial alliance meeting was a proposal to remove the name of Jesus Christ from all alliance documentation.

For the second month of consideration about this change, I was the only dissenting vote among the ministers. To me it was very apparent that Satan was blinding the eyes and hearts of many good men and women. Our church and family went into serious prayer that the Christians of the county would cause the ministers to retain Jesus Christ as the central purpose of the alliance of Christian ministers. After sixty days it was now time for the final vote.

Almost every minister had leaders with him or her, producing the largest attended meeting in the history of the alliance. Then to my utter amazement and great shock, after officially opening the meeting, the president of the alliance directly asked me to present the reasons that I had raised in the past two meetings for the defeat of the proposed change.

Filled with the Holy Spirit, I said what He gave me to say concerning the primary reasons for retaining the name of the Lord Jesus Christ in our organization documentation. While God's words came from me, there was obvious joy and relief demonstrated from the vast majority of the ministers and laymen present. Then one by one, as each cast their vote, the pastors agreed with me.

Several said that their personal position change came from the fact that their own members asked them to keep the name of Lord Jesus Christ in the documentation. One minister said that he was told by his board, "If you don't vote this way, your job is at stake."

Then with a complete reversal of the last two meeting's majority discussions, a strong majority approved the defeat of the previously popular proposal. This meant that the central purpose for the alliance would remain to bring glory, honor, and service to the Lord Jesus Christ. At that moment, the ministerial alliance united in stating that Jesus Christ is Lord indeed!

There was great relief and jubilation at the results. The only negative vote, which was not even voiced, would have come from the minister of the Latter-Day Saints, who loudly and with anger stormed out of the assembly.

Story #11–House Provision

Almighty God has provided several houses, buildings and ranches for us. Here is one story. It became obvious that our ranch was too much for me to oversee while I was serving as the pastor of spiritual counseling at our church. We listed the ranch property for sale and began taking all the normal steps for seeking another home. After several months with no sales contract, I turned to serious prayer. One Sunday morning I received the following message from the sermon: "There comes a time that our heavenly Father really expects us to get specific with Him about our needs."

Therefore, after church that morning, kneeling in the rear parking lot of the building, I was led to point to a house directly behind the building and prayed, "Dear Lord, what is wrong with that house for Donna and me? We really do need to get the housing matters settled. Please do Your will about our residence. In Jesus's name, amen." I did not tell Donna about my prayer.

The next morning when I was approaching my church office, I was led to turn down the street and look at the front of the house that I had prayed for the day before. Doing so, I noticed that a man was putting up a For Sale sign in the yard. I stopped and asked for the name of the real estate agent and if I might look at the house. He said that the owners were in the house and went to ask permission. I was the first to see the house, which instantly seemed like a fit for our needs. Later that day Donna looked at it and confirmed my opinion. Within three days the Lord provided a buyer for our ranch who paid in cash. Within two weeks all was done, and we were living in a beautiful house directly behind my place of work. Soon afterward, the church paved a sidewalk from our backyard to the church parking lot, by which countless numbers visited our home for twelve years.

Story #12– I Am the Thorn in Your Flesh, a Messenger of Satan

In my study was a very strong, excited, wide-eyed, twenty-five-year-old man speaking to me in a very loud voice, "You must take more time to talk with me about these doctrines. You are wrong about several things, and I am going to force you to see things the correct way, my way."

Filled by the Holy Spirit, in a firm, slow voice, I said, "Frank, as I said earlier, in obedience to the Word of God, I make it a practice not to argue or debate doctrines that bring hurt and division. You are trying to force me into such a situation and I simply will not go there. I have explained this to you several times, but you refuse to honor me. So, you need to leave my office now, for I have a lot of work that I must get done."

Then another spirit in the man exposed himself. As I looked into the window of his heart, I watched his eyes change. His eyes gave me advanced warning of the snarl that came next. "Brother JD, I am your personal thorn in the flesh, a messenger of Satan to bring you torment and pain. I will not leave until I am ready to leave. You cannot make me."

Of course, a spirit of fear was attempting to rise up within me, which I quieted quickly in the name of our Lord, Jesus Christ. Following the Holy Spirit's leadership in a calm and firm manner, I stood up and walked toward the door and said, "You evil spirit within Frank, I am speaking to you now. I am not speaking to Frank. In the name of Jesus Christ, my Lord, I tell you to follow me out this door and leave the church property right now. Frank, I am talking to you. If you do not leave, I will call Sheriff Jones and have you arrested as I have done to others before you."

With that, I opened the door and stepped outside. Frank kept talking in loud, abusive, uncooperative words as he walked by me. I shut the door and heard no more from him for many years.

Story #13– Instant Healing from Twenty Years of Allergies

In late August of 1978, the constant nasal draining and burning eyes were really tearing me up. Every season change since 1958 brought severe allergy reactions. After many medical tests the only relief came from self-injections of medication. Once I learned what God's Word said about the provisions of healing from the stripes of the Lord Jesus Christ, I was seriously interested in seeking His health.

Early one morning, after tossing and turning all night with constant nasal drainage and burning eyes, I got on my face on the farmhouse hallway floor. (I was quiet so that I did not wake the family.) I said, "Dear heavenly Father, I know that Your Word says that Christ has provided good health for me when I am obedient. Also, I know that most often the reason that your spiritual children are sick relates to some unresolved sin (Job 33:14, 19–30; 1 Corinthians 11:28–31; Revelation 2:21–24). Honestly, I do not know of any sin in my life that I have not dealt with You about. You and I both know that I have been consistently asking for Your healing. Well, it seems like You are the problem here and not me. However, of course, I know that the problem is me, not You. Anyway, if there is unconfessed sin, let me know about it, and I will come clean."

At that moment I heard the Holy Spirit's still, small voice say very clearly, "Are you finally serious about this?" Surprised but very earnest, I said right back, "Yes, Lord, I am serious. What sin is in me?"

Quickly came back the answer, "It is your sin of presumption that is your continuing problem." I said in response, "But Lord, I don't know of such. Show me my sin, and I will repent."

Again, quick as a wink came the answer in a full-color vision of a hot summer day in Long Beach, California, in 1963. The vision included the motorcycle siren, the jaywalking citation, and the very angry officer, who said these convicting words directly to me: "You presumptuous SOB! Don't you know you could have killed your whole family by jaywalking on this busy street? Use the crosswalks like law-abiding citizens."

Well, the vision nailed me. I fell on my face and cried out, "Oh, Lord, yes, I remember that very well. However, at that time I did not catch the word *presumptuous*. You are right. I promise to learn what this sin is and to stop every hint of it in my life. I am so sorry. Please forgive me in Jesus Christ's name."

My healing took place instantaneously as I came to wonderful peace. I stepped to the nearby bathroom and looked in the mirror. The red facial and neck skin was replaced with my normal complexion. The runny nose and watering eyes were also normal. I could not believe my reflection at that moment, but I praised Jesus Christ without waking anyone. I went back to bed and awoke refreshed in a few hours.

I waited all day to confirm the reality of the healing and described everything to the family at suppertime. It has now been thirty-six years since that miraculous healing. I have never had another allergy attack. A few times since then when a sniffle occurs to me, I quickly humble myself and ask the Lord to show me any sin, especially any form of presumption.

God's amazing sign and wonderful vision and instant healing have assisted many persons to identify what the heavenly Father is telling them. For more information, please see *Chapter 18, God's Four-Step Health Plan*, in this book.

Story #14–Job Offered without Personal Interviews

I received an honorable discharge from the US Navy in December 1963. As I began looking for a teaching job, I realized how difficult it was going to be to find an opening at midterm. The only school choir director job I found was in a west Texas town. This school district was the second highest paying system in Texas, but there was a problem that seemed insurmountable. The school had a policy that they never hired anyone without a personal interview. Of course, because of distance and time, there was no way that was going to happen.

This was another powerful move of God's hand in our lives. After the superintendent contacted the university I had attended, he made an exception because the school of music was known to be the best in the nation and my professors highly recommended me.

By mail, I signed and returned the contracts while I was still in California. When I was welcomed to assume duties, my principal said, "In my twenty years in the system I have never known anyone to be hired without having a personal interview. You came highly recommended, so we are expecting great things from you. Let me know of anything you need."

Public school music teaching was a great joy to me, and I was always blessed with exceptional students. I taught choir and orchestra for five years in elementary school and four years in junior high, and I served as high school choir director and music supervisor for four years. Donna taught elementary school for twenty-five years. From this beginning, Smith's Music Place on the city square offered full-line retail music services for twelve years.

Story #15–Money from Heaven

It was November 1979, and Donna's birthday was just a day away. I wanted to be able to give her a nice gift but doing so would really put a strain on our finances. In Jesus Christ's name, I shared my heart's desire with the heavenly Father that morning before daylight.

That evening Donna had prepared black eyed peas and corn bread for supper. After we had eaten, I helped clean the kitchen. We lived in an old farmhouse ten miles from town. The nearest inhabitants were approximately five miles away.

We had no sink disposal, so I went outside to the front porch to throw out the juice from the black-eyed peas. It was dark and very windy. As I tossed the juice in the air, I noticed that something fell to the ground as the juice hit it. I went to see what it was, and by the light from the porch, I saw a wet twenty-dollar bill lying on the ground. I could hardly believe my eyes.

In the next moment I heard that still, small voice say, "My son, you asked to be able to give Donna a gift. Here is My provision." On my knees I just wept and thanked Him for His great love and concern for His children.

Story #16–The Navy Gives a Second Chance

The US Navy Officer Candidate School presented seven courses, which I took in a four-month period amid a military protocol environment. At the end of the four-month period (September 1962), I did not have the passing GPA for the two courses, which required higher math and science skills. Donna and I were expecting the dreaded disgrace of failing OCS. Such failures always received the worst duty assignments in the US Navy. Several of my friends who had not passed OCS were now serving on icebreaker ships in faraway places. Donna and I, along with our families in Texas, prayed that God would provide for us or that I would be granted a rollback (a two-month opportunity to bring up the GPA.)

At the hearing, my OCS personnel records were read before the board. I fully expected to hear the worst when to my amazement an OCS instructor stood and asked to enter some "additional evidence concerning Officer Candidate Smith." He read the records of my exceptional guard duty during severe weather conditions and recommended a rollback, which the board so ordered. In the hall this senior chief said to me, "Well done, Smith, because of your faithful duty, you get a two-month rollback."

At this direct and timely intervention from almighty God, we worshipped the Lord Jesus Christ together upon our knees in our small apartment. As it turned out, the military service provided much real-world growth for me and introduced me to the criminal justice system.

As a presidential commissioned officer, my shore duties included what is now known as Judge Advocate General (JAG) and Naval Criminal Investigation Service (NCIS), which was almighty God's training for many years within the Texas Department of Criminal Justice Unit Chaplaincy and State Parole Residential Care from 1984 to 1999.

As an additional blessing, fifty-two years after my honorable discharge, Texas citizens invited me (and my son Jon, who was my trip guardian) on an all-expenses paid visit to the war memorials in Washington, DC, through Honor Flight of Fort Worth.

Story #17–On an Eighty-Degree Bright Spring Afternoon I Was Cold Enough to Shiver

The minister of the largest church in town welcomed us into his expansive, well-decorated office. Our host, who had many degrees and credentials, was in many people's eyes the most successful pastor in the county. We three ministers were present at the invitation of one of his members, a respected missionary who was also present during this meeting. Our team of veteran pastors was going to confront this young minister at the request of a missionary pastor from his own flock.

The subject was the proposed modification of the constitution and bylaws of the local county ministerial alliance, which our host pastor had written. As some of God's ministers in this county, we were concerned about the proposed changes.

When we mentioned his proposal to remove the name of Jesus Christ from the alliance documentation, I noticed a very strange physical coldness come upon me. It actually felt like someone had come into the room and mysteriously turned the thermostat very low. I marveled to myself that on an eighty-degree spring afternoon I was cold enough to physically shiver. The Holy Spirit inwardly counseled me to get ready. My spiritual senses were on high alert for directions from Jesus Christ through the Holy Spirit within my heart.

When the point was made that the removal of Jesus Christ within his latest and final version was a complete reversal from the first edition he had sent to us, I noticed that his eyes and demeanor changed considerably. Instead of being cordial, receptive, and professional, an adversarial position in body language and voice occurred from our host.

Suddenly, with curt abruptness, he stated that he didn't owe us any explanations. After boasting that a considerable majority of the county ministerial alliance would agree with what he had proposed, he began bringing our visit to a halt.

At that moment, the Holy Spirit prompted words and actions that served God's purpose. In calm power and cordial paternal expressions, I offered from our team several reasonable, prudent steps to return to his original written position and retain the name of Jesus Christ in the documents. His adamant refusal prompted my next words, "Brother, don't you want assistance to minister in true Christ-honoring ways instead of continuing down this path of falsehood and hypocrisy you began in both this church and the ministerial alliance?"

Finally, he answered, "No," and he ushered us out of his office. As our team visited after the meeting, we confirmed that we had just experienced spiritual warfare and agreed to be in strong prayer for this minister and the local Christian family.

Sadly, at that point this pastor stopped meeting with the area ministers, and from his pulpit spoke negatively about the minister alliance. Within a month his proposal to take Jesus Christ's name out of the alliance documentation was soundly defeated by the group. In addition, within four months, great emotional and spiritual harm within his family became public information as his marriage crumbled and he was forced to resign from the ministry.

Story #18–Pacific Ocean Vision

It was during a weeklong Pacific full squadron exercise between Long Beach, California, and Seattle, Washington, when this event took place. I was actually looking forward with excitement to several days at sea in the hopes of gaining my sea legs, and I reported for duty that special morning. No sooner had we gotten underway than I became ill. My vomiting continued as long as I was standing or sitting upright. I tried several times during the first two or three days to assume my duties, but with no success. I could eat a few crackers and get some water to stay down, but only if I was on my back. Rather than messing up spaces inside the ship, I spent as much time as possible above deck. The same physical reaction would occur if I was sitting or standing, so I would lay many hours on deck.

As I got weaker, my system began shutting down, causing the navy medic to suggest to the captain that I stay below deck on my back for several hours to prevent vomiting so that I could regain my strength.

Early the next morning in a serious effort to get my sea legs, I asked permission to be tied to the captain's chair. I thought I could push through my problem and attempt to give the other officers a rest. A commissioned officer had to be on duty at all times; however, in just a few minutes I was vomiting portions of my stomach lining and was in a great deal of pain.

At about 2:30 a.m. with no one around, I untied myself, climbed on to the top deck railing next to the captain's chair, and prepared to jump to the sea below. I had to stop the pain. I awaited the ship's starboard lurch so that my leap would cause me to miss each deck below. At that moment I was amazed at another powerful move of God's hand in my life. While I was looking at the black Pacific Ocean below me, the surface became a white movie screen on which I saw in full color my beautiful wife, Donna, holding our four-month-old son, Jon Alan. They looked so happy. They were smiling and laughing, and I wanted to be there with them.

Though I did not realize this in my weak condition, almighty God sent this vision to save my life. This vision caused me to stop what I was about to do, and at that moment I fainted and fell back, landing safely on the top deck. The noise brought assistance, and I awoke two days later at Bremerton Naval Base in Seattle, Washington.

The Naval Medical Department declared me unfit for sea duty and the Secretary of the Navy provided me shore duties to finish my military obligation. As it turned out, my work as a Naval Crime Scene Investigator and Courts Martial lawyer prepared me for many years of chaplaincy work within state institutions and safe house rehabilitation.

Story #19–Protection from Physical Harm

While working in a small engine repair shop, the Holy Spirit revealed a portion of God's plan for protection from physical harm. I worked in with another technician. This coworker and I had worked together for several months without a problem. One day at our workstations, which were approximately five feet apart, we casually spoke about something noncontroversial like the weather or results of a ball game. Looking at my project on the bench, my chin tilted and eyes down, I could see with my peripheral vision things to my side.

Suddenly I noticed to my complete surprise and alarm that my coworker was standing over me. His face was filled with wrath and violence. He was holding a large wrench in his hand, and it was raised above my head about to strike me. He had not made a sound or warning of any kind. For me things went in slow motion. In a split second I thought, *Why is he doing this? Do I fight or run?*

Then a very soft whisper inside me (nothing heard by my ears) said to me, "If your enemy strikes you on one cheek, turn to him the other cheek." Right then I understood that these were instructions from the Holy Spirit for this moment in time. In my attempt to obey the Holy Spirit's instructions, I slid to my knees on the floor, looked at the mechanic, took off my glasses, and said,

"Brother Bill, if you must hit me, do it, but remember that I love you and our Lord Jesus Christ loves you."

I was amazed to see the redness instantly drain out of his face. His arm fell to his side, and he dropped to the floor. I was completely shocked and filled with joy to see that my obedience to the Holy Spirit had brought such dramatic victory and that I was not hurt.

This sequence, of hearing a clear command from our Lord Jesus Christ, delivered by the Holy Spirit, and followed with my obedience, has been repeated for His glory many times.

Story #20–Red Fire Approximately Four Inches Long Came from Her Eye Sockets

While I was in the office of a minister, who was a well-respected vice president of the county ministerial alliance, I uncovered a lie that she had spoken. As I was gently but firmly attempting to suggest a way to proceed toward reconciliation, she became enraged, and another spirit from within her took control of her words, facial features, and her eyes in particular.

She then spewed out harsh, untrue, and irrational words, but her eyes were the tool used in an attempt to bring me into fear captivity. Her face was somewhat contorted but still recognizable as the same person as before, but there was red fire approximately four inches long coming from her eye sockets.

I quickly discerned this evil spirit was obviously of less strength than the Holy Spirit, who resided within me (1 John 4:4). I exercised the spiritual fruit of self-control and calmly used the words given to me at that moment by the Holy Spirit to end the conversation. I departed the office in peace and victory. The enemy within this local minister was exposed and brought into the light.

The next day her church secretary found a note saying, "I have an unexpected call from another state and must leave immediately." This caused much confusion to that congregation and the county ministerial alliance. As far as I know, no one ever heard from that minister again. The Holy Spirit confirmed within me that the kingdom of Jesus had received a victory in this all.

Story #21–Sale of Business and Commercial Building in a Depressed Economy

The chamber of commerce president, a longtime friend and prominent businessman, asked if he could buy me a cup of coffee. The purpose for the visit was revealed when he said, "JD, this is a very depressed financial time in our city as we all understand. I want to know how in the world you sold your music store now. Who would want to buy Smith's Music Place?"

This amazing sale of a retail business was a sign and wonder to a man who had an ear to hear and eyes to see what the Holy Spirit was doing in the Smith family. I told him that it was clearly the mighty hand of God at work in our lives as we attempted to obey the commands of God's Word. In the practical world we did nothing out of the normal.

He then asked me personal questions about how to get the same relationship with God in his life that I had in mine. With gentleness and respect I attempted to answer his question in terms he could understand, and he thanked me and paid for my coffee.

Two years later, the Lord God sent a commercial firm from Big Spring, TX to purchase our commercial building on the West side of the square. The same businessman bought me another cup of coffee, and asked the same question, "JD, no one is selling commercial property around the city square during this financial downturn. How in the world did you sell the Smith Building to a business from out of town?" My answer was the same, "Almighty God did this amazing deed as a part of His continual care for my family, since I do my part in obeying Matthew 6:33."

Story #22–Some of My Flock Turned Against Me

At a life group meeting in a member's home, a former minister who was one of our new church members, introducing a new doctrine before I got there. Before I arrived, he told the group that I would not accept his new teaching. Unknown to everyone at the meeting, he had spoken to another member who was ready to try to get me into an argument or debate over the doctrine.

Upon their first words, I discerned in my spirit that this was an attempt to divide the group. I said to everyone that the church elders would be happy to consider in depth the new teaching and report back.

My attempts to diffuse any argument among the group and to assist the life group to get on with that night's discussion were not quickly received. Some of my flock, including the associate pastor, turned against me during that evening and said some hurtful things. During this time the Holy Spirit provided me unusual inward peace and power to remain unstirred and to protect the flock from division. Despite these unrighteous attempts of the enemy of our souls in the use of precious persons, overall calm was maintained, and the evening concluded in peace.

The next day the associate pastor was convicted by the Holy Spirit of error, asked others and me for forgiveness, and was forgiven and restored. In a few weeks when we attempted to set a meeting with the elders to discuss the questionable new doctrine, this man would not do so. Then only a few months later this same man, a former minister, was convicted of criminal activities and forced by the state of Texas to relocate out of our county. One by one, most of the flock thanked me for my protection and received God's forgiveness from me. Overall, we lost no members and became stronger.

Story #23–The Mad Mechanic

Angry Andy was an excellent mechanic and a supervisor in the tractor dealership. However, as his name suggests, Andy had significant problems with anger management. I was working at my stall, rebuilding an engine for a ranch pickup, when Andy came to his stall across the building. It was near the front overhead tractor door. To my surprise, he raised the tractor door. It was snowing heavily on this winter morning, and the cold wind blowing in the large doorway was very uncomfortable. The doorway was very tall and wide for tractors and bulldozers to enter the shop area, and it allowed an enormous wind flow throughout the shop. There were five other mechanics on duty, and the big boss was out of town.

As one man who had not seen Andy went over and shut the overhead door, in frustration Andy would open it and cuss at the man. He even threw a tool at one of the men. I had enough sense not to close the tractor door, but I prayed for guidance as to what I should do in order to be a good worker. I put on my coat and gloves and did as much I could, but mechanic work requires free fingers and hands.

Around eleven o'clock Andy went to lunch. I was impressed by the Holy Spirit to sacrifice Donna's homemade cookies by giving them to Andy, but I did not want to. I thought of the verse, "Pray for and do good to your enemies." As soon as he left, I shut the overhead door and did as much work as I could. I figured he would be gone to lunch for an hour. Right before the hour was up, I chose to obey the Spirit's directive and put my cookies on his workbench with a short note, and then I left for lunch.

When I returned from lunch, I was saddened that the door was open again, but I was more concerned to see the cookies scattered across the floor near his workbench. I thought, *I guess I was deceived by a counterfeit spirit other than the Holy Spirit.* Therefore, from 2:00 p.m. to 5:00 p.m., I did as best I could in cold working conditions to finish the day.

At 5:00 p.m., only Andy and I were in the shop as I left. As I walked by him, Holy Spirit quickened me to say, "Well, Andy, it's been an interesting day. I hope you have a good evening." To my surprise, he turned, looked me squarely in the face, and said, "Thank you, Smith, for the cookies. I am sorry I threw them on the floor. I had a terrible night, and today has been no better." I said, "I'm sorry about your night. What happened?" He explained that his wife was dying with cancer and that he had gotten word after work yesterday of the finality of her health situation. It would be just a matter of time until she would be dead, and he was so distraught he did not know how to operate.

I suggested that we go to my truck, where for about an hour he received from me encouragement and the love of Jesus Christ. As he revealed many serious matters, we prayed about them in Jesus Christ's name. On my way back to the farmhouse, the Spirit said in His still, small voice, "JD, you did the correct thing with the cookies. Christ's love shown in the midst of anger was your key to the kingdom of God conversation that followed. Well done."

Story #24–Unexpected Inheritance

In the fall of 1982, my second cousin Vera called one morning and asked if I would do some tree trimming in her front yard. The next morning, with my equipment in my pickup, I drove the thirty miles to the nearby city and arrived about 7:00 a.m. Vera invited me in for a cup of coffee before I started the work.

Amazingly, it was 1:00 p.m. before I ever did any outside work, for you see, upon sitting down for the cup of coffee, Vera said, "Jon Dean, I have known you all of your life. I have always watched you and believe that your life proves your strong Christianity. I believe you can tell me the truth that I am longing to hear, and I will believe what you say because of your life. Many of my relatives through the years have begged me to join their church, saying it was better than another church. I have always been confused. Why is one church better than another church? I do not believe that those relatives know what they are saying.

Now as I am getting older, I want to know the truth about Jesus Christ and heaven. I will trust what you say because I know how you and Donna have lived. Jon Dean, you did not know it, but several of my teacher friends have told me what your family has done in your town all these years. Again, it proves who you are. In addition, you know that my dearly departed husband, Charlie, was a believer in God all of his life, but we did not go to church because I was against it.

Moreover, if there is a heaven, I want to be with Charlie there for eternity. You see, my daddy, whom I loved very much and was a wonderful dad, said to us children, 'Don't believe in Jesus Christ.

Christianity is just like Christmas and Santa Claus.' Daddy was one of the most respected men in the county and did a lot to help others all through his life. I trusted him and did not want to be disappointed in Jesus Christ like so many are about Santa Claus. So instead of being Christian and churchy, all of my life I have tried to be an honorable, kind, and gentle person. I have tried never to do anyone harm and to always be excellent in my lifestyle."

To my joy, I was able to answer Vera's serious questions by using her Bible to bring answers that she understood. On her knees with me at about eleven o'clock that morning, Vera asked Jesus Christ to be her personal Savior. Before I left town, I contacted a pastor and made an appointment for him and one of his members who had taught school with Vera for many years. Before she died a few years later, she enjoyed Christian fellowship with many friends and family.

Later, in 1984, after I resigned my teaching job to plant a church, almighty God's hand blessed us financially from Vera's estate. We knew nothing about being in her will, and we expected nothing. In all, this inheritance amounted to a little more than $28,000.

Later, as one of God's signs and wonders, one of Vera's sisters-in-laws told me, "Jon Dean, we were so blessed at how Vera welcomed your information and became a Christian. Even though our church teaches that you must be in our church to be saved, our family now believes that Vera became a true Christian thanks to your instruction and timely answers. We saw that you used her inheritance money to plant the church that love built. Our family took note that you spent your inheritance building God's kingdom rather than on yourself."

Story #25–Victory over Demonic Man in Café

I talked with the missionary pastor while Donna and his wife visited for an hour before we met for lunch. In answer to their questions, Donna and I stressed that a great spiritual struggle is always going on but is usually not seen by most American Christians. Prior to leaving our man-to-man time, I said to the minister, "Brother, I believe the Holy Spirit just said that something demonic will happen during lunch. Satan would like to steal the seed truths we are discussing, just as a raven picks up seed on a path. We must be alert to protect this from happening." He said okay, and we went to join our wives for lunch at the café.

While we were sitting around a table in the busy café, we were all involved in a serious conversation. We were affirming some deeper biblical truths, and this couple was really getting a good hold of concepts which made a lot of sense to them. I saw a man come in the café door and come directly toward us. He could have stopped to explain to anyone in the line of waiting people the reason that his face showed so much worry, pain, and very great need. However, he ignored more than a dozen people and headed straight toward us, which raised my spiritual discernment level. Led by the Holy Spirit, I said to the three of them, "Listen carefully. A man is coming this way who I can see clearly. Do not fear. We will be safe, but I tell you – do not make eye contact with him."

The four of us never looked directly at him but kept discussing our subject and ignored him. He stood approximately two feet from our chairs and waited for what seemed like a long time (probably forty-five seconds). Given spiritual insight, I could sense the moment his mission was defeated. At that moment he turned slowly around and walked out the door thirty feet away. As he left, we all heard his strange and guttural voice say, "You have a very nice day."

What the Holy Spirit had prompted me to tell the pastor ahead of time had come to pass. We were amazed at God's grace, our spiritual discernment, and the spiritual victory we had just received. Satan had sent one appearing to have great need to us pastors, and we would normally have stopped everything to help meet his great need. That, of course, would have stopped our conversation about spiritual warfare. But to the contrary, from hearing and following the Holy Spirit's direction, we were not deceived or hindered in our discussion about spiritual warfare. God received a great victory as the four of us observed these matters.

We praised the Lord Jesus together as we recalled that the Holy Spirit had told us in advance to be on spiritual alert. This story has been used again and again to demonstrate victory in spiritual warfare.

Story #26–"What Did You Say that Caused His Heart Attack?"

The senior prison official had asked me to create a program that would pull the various church ministry groups together. One church taught that only their members were getting into heaven. This was causing problems between the inmates. That church ministry was also breaking state laws by regulating ministry in prisons. The prison minister of that church would not respond to my attempts to visit with him. After a special prayer to be filled with the Holy Spirit, I called this prison minister to try once more to meet with him. During the conversation I said, "We are serving the same Lord Jesus Christ, aren't we? Will you at least meet me for breakfast tomorrow morning?"

At that very moment I heard him cough very heavily and feebly say, "Yes, I'll be there." He then hung up.

Two days later, after he missed the breakfast, I spoke with his wife on the phone. When she answered, she said, "Mr. Smith, you must have said something awful to my husband because when he hung up from talking with you, we had to rush him to the hospital. What did you say to my husband that caused him to have a heart attack?"

I answered her by relating my questions to her husband along with his answer. All she said was, "Thank you, Mr. Smith."

That ministry continued to violate the law within prison ministry. After he was warned repeatedly, the main prison minister was suddenly killed in a car crash, and within two months the local minister and his church were officially banned from the local prison for several years. The Holy Spirit had warned them in many ways, but they would not listen. The minister who had the heart attack never relented from the illegal prison actions and remained in frail health until he passed away.

Story #27–The White Dove Caravan

After God suddenly and expectantly stopped our freight company, I attempted to sell the fleet of used trucks. One sold rather quickly, but no matter what I did in attempts to sell the remaining six trucks, nothing worked. Four months later we had removed a portion of the backyard fence at our home and parked the trucks very close together, awaiting God's solution. One night near midnight, I was on my face near our garage, saying, "Dear Father, I just don't know what to do next. These trucks must be sold, and You must show me how. I do not know of any known sin in my life to confess to You. I want to be completely right with You on every matter of life. It is completely up to You. I give You this weighty load. Please do something."

The next morning in our kitchen a Christian campground ministry from another state was on TV. During breakfast the Holy Spirit whispered to me, "Look at all of the construction going on there. You should consider offering them your trucks for a fair price in a letter today." Before the mail went out, I obeyed the Holy Spirit's suggestion and mailed the letter.

About a week later our daughter Pamela called me at work and said, "Dad, I have the name and phone number of a man from another state who wants to talk with you about your trucks." When contacted, the vice president in charge of construction at the campground said, "Mr. Smith, for four months we have been looking for used trucks just like you describe in your letter. As a matter of fact, my son works for a large truck dealer here and has not been able to get us any such trucks."

We talked a couple of times during the next few days and agreed upon a fair deal. To our wonder and joy, several of our Christian friends along with my parents volunteered to drive them, at their own expense, from Louisiana to North Carolina. In two weeks with some help, we painted the white dove caravan, and the six-vehicle fleet was off. Some amazing adventures of near wrecks and angelic protections caused us to have prayer several times during the four-day round trip.

In addition, there were wonderful financial steps before, during, and after the trip that clearly showed God's intervention. It turned out that this was God's way to return us to the west Texas area for more than twenty years of kingdom building.

Story #28–Al Smith Came to Peace with God

My mom, Mattie Lee Richardson Smith, died in May of 1999, after which my dad, Albert Curlee (Al) Smith, invited Donna and me to leave Snyder and move to the Acorn Acres ranch to assist him.

During his last three months, as Al's physical system slowly began shutting down, a care team provided full-time comfort with a hospice team assisting in his final two weeks. I was on duty with him the night his life on earth ended and he underwent his graduation to heaven in March of 2000.

As his physical system was stopping, Al's mental, emotional, and spiritual functions were being greatly blessed by almighty God. In late January, Al said, "Jon Dean, I cannot figure out why I don't go ahead and die. Would you please help me find out why I am not at peace with God?" I agreed and began praying for spiritual insight. Soon the Holy Spirit provided four specific points to discuss with him. As we discussed these matters, Al chose to obey God's commands as I suggested them. Obedience to God brought peace to Al.

In about three weeks' time, Al's obedience to God's Word on the Holy Spirit's four points brought significant, noticeable change to him. His adult grandchildren, great-grandchildren, nephews, nieces, longtime friends, and caregivers commented to Donna and me about Al's change of demeanor, countenance, words, and actions. After this major event, Al just kept acknowledging to everyone that Jesus was wonderful and expressed kindness, gentleness, and sweetness to everyone around him.

Why Does Al Shake So Much When JD Lifts Him from Bed?

Al agreed that it was unreasonable for him to shake with fear each time I lifted him, but he could not stop himself. They prayed that God would explain the reason for this fear. Next the Holy Spirit reminded me of the fun story that Al often told, in which the grandfather dropped a little boy. Al's punch line was, "That will teach you not to trust anyone, not even your own father," and it always included Al's strange smile in his facial expression. I was led by the Holy Spirit to question Al, "Dad, it appears that you do not trust your own son. Do you really trust any man, and more importantly, do you really trust God? In addition, if not, why not, for you have been a very active church leader for more than sixty years?"

This question released the story of personal bitter roots from precious ninety-year-old Al Smith. Moreover, the results up to this point in his life showed that eighty years of religion about Jesus Christ had never brought Al into a relationship with Jesus Christ. This was the root of Al's shaking fear. At the age of twenty, Al was lied to and swindled by four men he knew very well—the school superintendent, his own pastor, the son of the pastor, and Al's father.

At high school graduation, either Al or the local pastor's son would receive the valedictorian scholarship. In a meeting called by the school superintendent, Al, the pastor, and his son were told that official word from the state education agency must arrive before the college scholarship funds could be released. About a week later Al received his own copy of the state education agency letter in the mail, which confirmed Al Smith as the highest scholastic ranking senior that year. Therefore, Al went to the school official to collect the cash award that would pay for his college fees.

To Al's horror, he received these words from the school superintendent: "Yes, Al, I received the original letter from Austin and confirm your own conclusions to expect the cash. However, I gave the cash scholarship to the pastor's son instead of you because his family is very influential, and everyone expected him to receive it. After all, your folks are just poor farmers, and no one really expected you to get the award. Therefore, officially you are this year's salutatorian, not the valedictorian. Now this meeting is over. Good day."

Al shared his disappointment, sadness, and anger at home with his family. Soon afterward, Al's father gave him hope by saying, "Well,

The Hidden Truth

son, I'll help you go to college anyway. You stay home this year, break up the fields, plant, harvest, and get the cotton crop to the gin, and I will give you a better award than the one you were cheated out of. You do this year's farming for me, and this team of matched young mules and the first bale of cotton you produce will be yours for college, I promise." But about seven months later when the cotton crop was ready for harvest, Al learned from the town banker that all of his dad's livestock, farmland, and crop production for several years to come belonged to the bank for unpaid debts. In truth, Al would not be receiving anything from the seven months of labor. Al had never known these facts. Therefore, lied to and swindled once again, this time by his own father, twenty-one-year-old Al devised and worked out his own survival plan.

Al did not return to the family house, but he quietly worked all night pulling cotton bolls. Then in early morning at the cotton gin, he got $100 for a bale of cotton, left the team and wagon at the gin, and caught the morning freight train to the nearby college town. He never discussed any of this with his dad or anyone else. Therefore, for almost seventy years he had personally justified taking the cotton money as his own deserved reward for being swindled and lied to. In addition, at that point he had set his personal life motto: "Never trust anyone, not even your own father."

Now on his deathbed, Al very seriously wanted to get right with God. At ninety, he fully realized that his many years of religious activity as church deacon had not actually prepared him. He was now ready to hear my Holy Spirit-provided words of life and spirit. "Dad, when you stand before almighty God face-to-face and the book containing your life records are open for all to see, will the cotton money be yours, or will it belong to the bank? Before you answer, remember who the judge is. Your answer could affect your own eternal life." Confronted with his coming death and judgment, Al Smith talked in detail with me about many things in his lifetime. Al began to realize the following:

- He had no peace with God at the time of his approaching death.

- His hard work and sacrificial honesty and integrity during the Great Depression did not help.
- His service in World Wars I and II, Korea, and Vietnam did not help him.
- His honest, hardworking, high professional honors and publications did not help him.
- His establishment of Meals on Wheels, the senior center, Retired Teachers Chapter, and the Pecan Valley MHMR centers did not help him.
- Weatherford College's Man of the Year Award did not help him.
- His considerable cash and real estate did not help him.
- His public belief statement of Jesus Christ's birth, death, burial, and resurrection as a young teenager had not made him ready.
- His water Baptism in the name of the Father, the Son, and the Holy Spirit had not prepared him for this moment.
- His regular eating of the Lord's Supper for all these years had not prepared him.
- More than seventy years of church work (faithful attender, tither, choir member, teacher, and active deacon) was not helping now.

Nothing Al Smith ever experienced had prepared him to meet God. Al was religious, but not in relationship with Lord Jesus Christ. So, he had no peace with God. Al asked me to assist him in getting down on his knees by his deathbed so he could bow before almighty God. While he was on his knees, Al confessed these and other sins, repenting and begging almighty God's forgiveness. He then pleaded to Jesus Christ to become his personal Savior and entrance door into the New Covenant leading to eternal life with almighty God.

At that very moment a great change began in Al Smith's life that all could see. God's great joy and peace from entering into His new covenant began showing immediately. These fantastic changes came from the new covenant provision of the Holy Spirit inside Al's new heart (Jeremiah 31:31–34; Ezekiel 36:25–27; Roman 8:14–16; Galatians 4:6–7, 5:22–26).

Al's Break from Secret Organization

Another fact that the Holy Spirit brought to me had to do with Al's fifty years in a men's secret organization, which God sees as false worship. Al instructed me to gather and destroy by fire all of his organization's paraphernalia, records, plaques, books, emblems, rings, aprons, etc. Al then prayed, "Dear God Almighty, in the name of Jesus Christ, please forgive me from my false worship in these idol temples. I now break all vows, pledges, and connections with this secret society. I officially state my personal will and choice to abandon, leave, and depart all known practices of this false worship forever. I now demand all spirit forces from this false worship to depart from me, my house, and everything I possess. Never return! This is declared in the name of the Lord Jesus Christ, the King of Kings and Lord of Lords."

Again, from his repentance and obedience to God's will, new levels of personal peace with God and joy within were received. Al Smith's countenance became one of joy and peace and gentleness.

Al Confesses Sinful Financial Practices

Regarding the misuse of his finances, Al recalled Christ's parable of the man who tore down barns and built bigger ones to store his wealth. Al admitted that he was that same kind of fool because he had hoarded (stored up) his money instead of trusting almighty God to be his provider in all ways and in all times. He confessed using money incorrectly. Al was convicted of his failure to use his finances for God-honoring things for many years.

Again, I witnessed Al ask almighty God to forgive him for his financial sins and idolatry of material things in the name of Lord Jesus Christ. One morning Al gathered Donna, me, his adult grandchildren and their spouses, and his great-grandchildren around his bed and said, "I have been wrong for hoarding and storing up money instead of trusting almighty God to be my provider at all times. Do not make the sinful mistake I did." Al received more peace from God.

Al Forgives Others

Another matter was for Al to correctly understand God's definition of what He meant by forgiving one another. Al thought if he forgave someone an offense, it would be the same as saying, "The offense never occurred." However, he learned that God said these things about forgiveness:

"I will be merciful and gracious toward their sins and I will remember their deeds of unrighteousness no more" (Hebrews 8:12 AB).

"For as you forgive people their trespasses [their reckless and willful sins, leaving them, letting them go, and giving up resentment], your heavenly Father will also forgive you. Nevertheless, if you do not forgive others their trespasses [their reckless and willful sins, leaving them, letting them go, and giving up resentment], neither will your Father forgive you your trespasses" (Matthew 6:14–15 AB).

Therefore, Al forgave the four men who had hurt him. He said, "Dear Lord God, I forgive [each man's name] for his sin of [identified the sin] against me. I ask You to forgive and bring [each man's name] into Your New Covenant. Thank You, Lord Jesus, for forgiving me since I have chosen to obey Your command to forgive everyone who sinned against me. I make this prayer in the name of my Savior, the Lord Jesus Christ, amen."

Family and friends witnessed Al's complete peace for the last weeks of his life. One evening while he was peacefully sleeping, he gently passed away while I sat beside him.

There is more to this story. Another person who saw the peace with God that Al Smith received was his family's longtime caregiver. At her next job she talked to her patient, who was a believer in Jesus Christ, about the amazing peace with God that Al had received. This patient and his wife were acquainted with Al and Mattie Smith and knew about me. Soon thereafter, Donna and I were invited to the home of this family. Once again almighty God, through the powerful Holy Spirit, provided peace with God, in the name of King Jesus

Christ. I presented the most common categories of sins of God's people found in excerpts from 1 Corinthians 10:6–13:

- "Do not be idolaters." Do not put anything more important than God.
- "Do not commit sexual immorality." Do not indulge immoral thoughts or deeds.
- "Do not test the Lord." Do not knowingly refuse to do God's will.
- "Do not grumble." Do not complain about situations or circumstances.

As the critically ill man evaluated these four common sins, the Holy Spirit convicted him about his own sins. In front of three witnesses, he confessed his guilt and shame about these sins to the heavenly Father in the name of the Lord Jesus Christ. He declared that he would never do these sins again and asked almighty God for forgiveness of these matters.

With tears of rejoicing at the cleansing of his conscience and removal of the heaviness in his heart, he received great peace with almighty God. He expressed his appreciation strongly to us. A few days later he passed away in peace.

The amazing story of Al Smith's courageous actions has blessed many. He took ownership of his sin convictions from the Holy Spirit. He begged almighty God's forgiveness in Jesus Christ's name. Jesus Christ became his personal payment in full for his sin and guilt. On his deathbed he entered the narrow door into the kingdom of God. Amen.

Story #29 – 700 Students Experience Five Years of Peace and Excellence

As the elementary music teacher for the 700-student school on the poor side of town, I normally taught classes of thirty students. However, on Fridays, ninety students (three combined classes) joined me on the auditorium stage for a 30-minute music class. These combined classes provided me some extra preparation time for the next week.

Being a Kindergarten through Sixth Grade Campus, the normal student ages were from five through twelve years old, with the exception being "the boys who shaved". These five or six boys in the sixth grade had failed several years and were classified as troubled students. A large percentage of our students in all classes were taking medications for emotional disorders.

From my daily applying the spiritual tools described in *Chapter 18, Three Power Authorizations,* this student body annually produced outstanding choirs and orchestras for five consecutive years. The powerful results of consistent student peace and excellence of voices and instruments received notice from many sources. The local teaching staff and student parents spread statements like this, "We are so proud of our school choir and orchestra. You have got to come hear them." The senior school system administrators brought the Texas Education Agency representatives to observe a normal school pit orchestra that performed at every school assembly.

During these five years, the fact that not one child had to leave the music classroom for disciplinary actions caught the attention of several teachers who privately asked me, "Why is it that all of our students, even the most troubled ones, become peaceful and very productive when they are with you?" It was local schoolteachers that started coming to our home on Sunday afternoons to get answers. From this came the first of several plantings of "the church that love built".

Story #30 – 1300 Prisoners Enjoy the State's Most Peaceful Prison

In the fall of 1989, the state prison chaplain in our county invited me to teach Christian hymns and worship choruses to the prison church. From my daily applying the spiritual tools described in *Chapter 18, Three Power Authorizations,* the following amazing God story came to pass.

The Hidden Truth

After I received confirmation from my spiritual advisers, I agreed to labor in the prison. During that year strong relationships were established among approximately fifteen inmates who faithfully joined me around the chapel piano for weekly praise and worship time.

As I began to know the men, I desired to teach them God's Word, but I limited my labor to my assignment, the music of the church. I chose to obey their authority and said nothing about my desire but committed it to the Lord in serious prayer. As a complete surprise (in answer to my prayer) at the end of the year, the chaplain said, "Brother JD, I have been seeking for more than twelve years but cannot find materials that produce mature believers in either the free world or the prison churches. With my large number of resources, denomination, nondenominational, and charismatic publications, I am not pleased with the results of any of these materials. I have seen the results of your labors at the church you planted in town. Would you pray about developing a weekly course at our prison that will produce mature Christians for life outside the prison?"

The Holy Spirit revealed to us what we have called the five basic subjects that Jesus Christ taught the twelve apostles. These same materials are presented in detail in Part 3 of this book.

Also, the other major success factor was to come into complete unity as Jesus described in John 17:20–23. We deliberately attempted to stop all arguing and competing that divides the local body of Jesus Christ. Anytime a fuss or debate began, it was quickly stopped. We attempted to help each man to become like Jesus Christ in the earth by learning to obey everything that Jesus Christ taught His twelve apostles.

"Therefore go and make disciples of all nations, baptizing them in the name of the Father and of the Son and of the Holy Spirit and teaching them to obey everything I have commanded you. And surely I am with you always, to the very end of the age" (Matthew 28:20).

Almost twenty-five years later, we continue to give much glory to God, as we saw the Free World Life Class change the spiritual environment of that state prison. These classes were so effective that in the mid-1990s, each individual who checked the box labeled, "Christian faith" on their prison interview form were invited by the chaplains to visit one of the classes. Soon the lives of members of the Free World Life Class changed their world, as these men lived out Christ's likeness in their workplaces and dorms. Eventually three classes met weekly with approximately eighty men attending.

The campus level of peace and calmness increased because of so many finding their own soul rest from the relationships with their changed friends. The standard answer to the question "What changed you?" became "Come see for yourself." In addition, the personal lives of many security officers were changed, including veteran senior officials who became Christians. When the prison security department went eleven months without filing a conduct infraction report to the state prison headquarters, heads began to turn. Even the governor of the state sent a secret inquirer to investigate the unit.

This prison informally became the most peaceful unit in the state. Almost twenty-five years later, inmates and their families still speak of this prison as "the nice prison unit". From those curriculums, we published *The Disciple's Journal* in 1995 which has been used throughout the world.

In 2018, a dear disciple friend since 1990 brought us the wonderful report that the Silent Gospel is still working strongly in this state prison. We join with you in giving heavenly Father all glory for His marvelous love for all humanity.

Co-Authors' Conclusions

We have been blessed beyond description by almighty God our heavenly Father and want you to get to know Him in the same way that we know Him.

Lord Jesus Christ is such a wonderful older brother and perfect example of faithful obedience to every task that our Father presented Him, the most difficult to become the guilt-payment for the sins of the world. What a blessing to have Him as our ever-present High Priest.

Holy Spirit, our daily companion and Kingdom of God Guide living within our hearts is such a deep friend who is always available for sharing rich, powerful truth on every matter.

Our disciples bring us continued earth-joy as they live out the God-truths that Holy Spirit inspired us to example and teach them to obey.

Jon Dean and Donna Smith

About the Authors

Married in 1962, Texans Jon Dean (JD) Smith and Donna Smith raised two children and are life partners in everything they do. Whether as musicians, teachers, ministers, or small business owners, JD and Donna labored to find God's truth and share it with others.

JD and Donna served on twelve church staffs, planted four churches, and established six state prison discipleship centers. For many years, the Smiths opened their homes and hearts, offering their love, time, and resources to people in need of practical, emotional, and spiritual support.

Until late 2019, the Smiths continued to teach and disciple others, from pastors to parents. Donna is challenged with advanced Parkinson's and JD is in the final stage of his earthly race. Both continue to praise God, enjoy true soul rest, minister to caregivers, and remain in rich relationship with family and friends.

A note from Lynn Baber:

This print edition of *The Hidden Truth* releases in January 2020. Today, January 5, 2020, I pray JD will remain on this side of eternity long enough to hold a copy in his hand.

"Thy will be done on earth as it is in heaven."

~

For questions, information, or comment, please email

lynn@LynnBaber.com

www.ingramcontent.com/pod-product-compliance
Lightning Source LLC
Chambersburg PA
CBHW072001110526
44592CB00012B/1171